PENGUIN PASSNOTES

The Go-Between

Dr Graham Handley has taught and lectured for over thirty years. He was Principal Lecturer in English and Head of Department at the College of All Saints, Tottenham, and Research Officer in English, Birkbeck College, University of London. He is a part-time lecturer in Literature with the University of London Department of Extra-Mural Studies, and has examined at all levels from C.S.E. to university honours degree. He has published on Dickens, Mrs Gaskell and George Eliot among others, and has edited *The Mill on the Floss* and *Wuthering Heights* for Macmillan and *Daniel Deronda* for the Clarendon Press. He is the author of the study guides on *To Kill a Mockingbird* and *The Pardoner's Tale* in the Penguin Passnotes series, as well as the Masterstudies of *Vanity Fair* and *Barchester Towers*.

PENGUIN PASSNOTES

L. P. HARTLEY
The Go-Between

GRAHAM HANDLEY
ADVISORY EDITOR: S. H. COOTE M.A., PH.D

PENGUIN BOOKS

Penguin Books Ltd, Harmondsworth, Middlesex, England
Viking Penguin Inc., 40 West 23rd Street, New York, New York 10010, U.S.A.
Penguin Books Australia Ltd, Ringwood, Victoria, Australia
Penguin Books Canada Limited, 2801 John Street, Markham, Ontario, Canada L3R 1B4
Penguin Books (N.Z.) Ltd, 182–190 Wairau Road, Auckland 10, New Zealand

First published 1987

Made and printed in Great Britain by
Richard Clay (The Chaucer Press) Ltd, Bungay, Suffolk
Filmset in Monophoto Ehrhardt

The publishers are grateful to the following Examination Boards for permission to
reproduce questions from examination papers used in individual titles in the Passnotes
series:

Associated Examining Board, University of Cambridge Local Examinations Syndicate,
Joint Matriculation Board, University of London School Examinations Department,
Oxford and Cambridge Schools Examination Board, University of Oxford Delegacy of
Local Examinations, Southern Universities Joint Board.

The Examination Boards accept no responsibility whatsoever for the accuracy or method
of working in any suggested answers given as models.

For Sandra, with love

Contents

Acknowledgements

I should particularly like to acknowledge the help of Eric Brown of Thames Polytechnic for drawing my attention to two interesting articles on *The Go-Between*, and for his own stimulating written commentary on the novel. I should also like to thank Gill Curtis for a critical reading of my typescript and for making a number of helpful suggestions.

The publishers acknowledge with gratitude the co-operation of Hamish Hamilton Ltd, publishers of *The Go-Between* in hardback.

To the Student

This book is designed to help you with your O-level, C.S.E. or 16+ English Literature examination. It contains a synopsis of the plot, a glossary of the more unfamiliar words and phrases, and a commentary on some of the issues raised by the text. An account of the writer's life is also included for background.

Page references are to the Penguin edition of the novel.

When you use this book remember that it is no more than an aid to your study. It will help you to find passages quickly and perhaps it will give you some ideas for essays. But remember: *This book is not a substitute for reading the text and it is your knowledge and your response that matter.* These are the things the examiners are looking for, and they are also the things that will give you the most pleasure. Show your knowledge and appreciation to the examiner, and show them clearly.

Introduction: L. P. Hartley, Life and Works

Leslie Poles Hartley was born on 30 December 1895 and was brought up at Fletton Tower near Peterborough in Northamptonshire. His father was a country solicitor who prospered, retired early, and obtained a further source of income when he became the owner of a brickworks. Leslie's mother was a quietly-spoken woman of apparently retiring nature but with a marked force of personality. Leslie was the only son. He had two sisters, and during their childhood they spent periods of time at Hunstanton. This was the original location for *The Shrimp and the Anemone*, the first part of Hartley's celebrated *Eustace and Hilda* trilogy.

Hartley was educated at Harrow and at Balliol College, Oxford. His education was interrupted by the First World War (1914–18), in which he served as a second lieutenant in the Norfolk Regiment. During his time at Oxford he became joint editor of the literary magazine *Oxford Outlook*. Although he was middle-class himself he moved easily in upper-class society, but his awareness of difference in manners and conventions and of the distances between the various classes was always to remain with him. These differences are seen clearly in Leo's experiences at Brandham Hall in the hot summer of 1900.

Hartley learnt the craft of writing by studying and absorbing the practice of other writers. Having obtained his degree in 1922, he became a reviewer for *The Spectator* and continued to write reviews for papers and journals until the 1950s. He spent some time each year until the Second World War in Venice, and it is perhaps not surprising that his first novel was set there. *Simonetta Perkins* (1925) is like *The Go-Between* in that the heroine tries to cross a barrier – of race; in *The Go-Between* the barrier is class. She loves, though she does not express it, a handsome gondolier (a man who rows a gondola on the Venetian canals). It comes to nothing. By contrast, Marian in *The Go-Between* expresses her passion for Ted; it comes to tragedy.

Although Hartley published two volumes of short stories in 1924 and 1932, it was not until 1944 that he issued *The Shrimp and the Anemone*. The treatment of childhood in this novel is a subtle psychological probing of children's reactions: fear, possessiveness, insecurity and, occasionally, joy. There are parallels with *The Go-Between*, between the boy Eustace and the boy Leo as well as the man Eustace and the man Leo. Hartley became prolific, producing the next two volumes of the *Eustace and Hilda* trilogy in 1946 and 1947. The work was widely and seriously acclaimed, and it brought Hartley into the front rank of English novelists. *The Boat* (1949) was followed by *The Go-Between* (1953) which, as Margaret Drabble has remarked, in the 'portrayal of leisurely Edwardian England, with its cricket matches, bathing parties, and lurking social embarrassments, is masterly'. Two years after *The Go-Between* Hartley brought out *A Perfect Woman*, while in 1957 he published *The Hireling*. This has class difference as part of its emphasis. The chauffeur Leadbitter falls in love with his regular client – the young, widowed Lady Franklin. She cannot take his advances seriously and prefers instead someone of her own social class who is morally unworthy of her.

It is not my intention to examine in detail either Hartley's novels or his many short stories, but one novel – *The Brickfield* (1964) – has distinct connections with *The Go-Between*. An ageing author confides to his younger male secretary the events of his childhood-cum-adolescence. He had been in love with a girl who, scared by her new governess into believing that she is pregnant, drowns in the pool in the brickfield. He finds her and, though he later becomes a successful novelist, the guilt of this incident warps his life. The connections with *The Go-Between* are (a) the shared technique of using a first-person narrator and (b) of showing how youthful experience becomes the malignant growth of guilt in maturity.

Hartley died in 1972. Well before his death, book-length critical studies as well as articles had begun to appear. One critic, Paul Blomfield, has pointed out Hartley's concern for the individual who is dominated by one feeling or idea to the exclusion of others. Leo is dominated by spells, by Marian and, after his experience at Brandham Hall, by feelings of guilt. Hartley is not so much a moralist as a writer who presents us with situations and leaves us as readers to judge their effects and what comment they are making on life, if any. Through his narrator in *The Go-Between* he explores Leo's consciousness, his thoughts, his reactions, his emotions, his fears. He places him in a number of situations in what Frederick R. Karl has called a world of 'upper middle-class gentility'. Hartley's view of that world is often a critical one. He reveals it to us through the impressions it made on a boy.

Hartley's writing is true to life. He has a sure insight into character, and presents it with consistency, revealing motive and action, thought and speech and inward emotion. He rouses expectation in his readers by making us want to know what actually happened during those very hot three weeks in 1900. *The Go-Between* is a clear investigation of that time, full of description, atmosphere, convincing dialogue, literary devices like the symbol (see pages 84–6 for definition), and imagery which give the novel its artistic effects. Above all, the reader of *The Go-Between* will enjoy the novel because it is a good story which compels our interest through to the end.

Synopsis of The Go-Between

In 1952 Leo Colston, who is in his sixties, comes across his old diary. At first he is reluctant to open it, but when he does he finds the date 1900, which is encircled by zodiac signs. Leo recalls how, bullied at school, he used curses against his tormentors, two of whom fell from the school roof that night. The other boys credited Leo with supernatural powers as a result. Turning through the diary, Leo discovers the notes he made of the summer holiday spent at Brandham Hall, home of his school friend Marcus Maudsley. The holiday proved disturbing and influenced Leo's future development; he decides, despite his fears, to recall everything he can about that period. He wants to discover how his subsequent life was affected by his boyhood experiences.

Leo's story now begins. He is an only child, living with his widowed mother near Salisbury. He has been much happier at school during the summer term, and an outbreak of measles at school has been attributed to his magical powers. He is invited to Brandham Hall, nearly backs out at the last moment, but goes on 9 July. He is met at Norwich and driven to the hall. He finds that he is to share a room with Marcus. After a few days he becomes drawn to Marcus's beautiful sister Marian. He is also fascinated by finding a deadly nightshade plant in a derelict outhouse.

A heatwave begins on 10 July. Leo himself had forecast that the weather would not be hot, and has brought unsuitable clothes. He casts a spell to lower the temperature, but this fails. Marian suggests that she takes him to Norwich the next day to buy him some light summer clothes. Mrs Maudsley objects, but Marian has her way. After buying the clothes they have lunch. Then Marian leaves Leo for an hour; he visits the cathedral and, when he returns, sees her in the distance saying goodbye to a man. Leo's clothes are displayed at the hall – his green suit evokes witty, punning comments – and on the next day there is a bathing party. Leo learns that Trimingham is to arrive that evening and that Mrs Maudsley wants Marian to marry Trimingham. He apparently has a badly scarred face as a result of being wounded in the Boer War. At the bathing place Leo sees Ted Burgess, a local tenant farmer. On the way back Leo saves Marian's dress from getting wet: he has not swum himself, and he puts his unused bathing suit around her neck to dry her hair. Marian seems very happy, and Leo too is happy at being able to help her.

On Sunday Leo meets Trimingham and is fascinated by the war wounds on his face. Meanwhile Marcus is ill, almost certainly with measles. On the way to church Leo accompanies Marian. Trimingham catches them up. Leo studies the tablets in church and later, in conversation with Trimingham, he realizes that Trimingham is the ninth viscount. The latter asks Leo to tell Marian that he has her prayer-book, but she does not respond. This is the first instance of Leo being employed as messenger or go-between. Later Leo goes out to explore, comes to a farmyard, climbs a straw-stack, slides down it and cuts his knee. The farmer, who is Ted Burgess, is angry with him but changes his tune when he realizes that Leo comes from the hall. He bandages Leo's knee. Leo offers to do anything for him in return, and Ted gives him a letter for Marian which must be kept secret. Leo goes back to the hall, praises Ted, and then gives Marian the letter. She too binds him to secrecy. He is a go-between, aware of the class difference between farm and hall, but innocent of the sexual love between Ted and Marian.

On one of Mrs Maudsley's suggested excursions Trimingham refers to Leo as Mercury (the messenger of the gods). Later, when they return to the hall, Leo records the temperature (94 degrees) after reading a letter from his mother, to which he replies. At Trimingham's request he goes to find Marian to ask her to join in the croquet (see Glossary 1). He meets her near the outhouses (see Glossary 1) where the deadly nightshade is, and eventually persuades her to join the other guests. Marian, who says she knows little of Ted, asks Leo to take a letter from her to the farmer.

The almost intolerable heat has now set in. On Friday Marcus is well enough to be allowed up. Leo feels that this will prevent him carrying any more messages (he will not have the freedom which he has had), but Marian gives him a note which she hasn't had time to seal up. He takes it to the farm. On the way his curiosity gets the better of him. He does not open it, but is able to read the words under the unsealed flap, and realizes that it is a love-letter from Marian to Ted. Leo, upset, delivers the letter to Ted but says that he cannot carry any more because of Marcus's recovery. Ted tells him that a mare is in foal, the conversation leads to 'spooning' (making love), and Ted promises to define this for the anxious Leo if he will continue to carry messages to Marian.

Saturday is the day of the cricket match (the hall against the village), with Leo acting as twelfth man (see Glossary 1) for the hall. The match is to be followed by a concert and Trimingham uses Leo as messenger to Marian, asking if she will sing 'Home, Sweet Home' that evening. The hall team bat, and are saved by a disciplined, restrained innings by Mr Maudsley, who makes 50 himself and sees his side to the respectable total of 142.

At first all goes well for the hall team, their bowlers being successful, but with the arrival of Ted Burgess at the wicket things begin to change (Leo notes the excitement of Marian). Ted scores 50 runs powerfully, and then one of his big hits injures a fielder; Leo as twelfth man comes on to the field. Trimingham puts himself on to bowl and, with three runs needed to win, Ted mishits and Leo makes a brilliant catch to get him out. He apologizes to Ted, but the latter generously praises him; Marian, greatly moved, remains with head bowed as the teams return to the pavilion. At the concert that evening Ted eventually agrees to sing and is accompanied at the piano by Marian. Afterwards Leo sings, enjoys a triumph, is ecstatically happy with Marian, and later half hears her singing 'Home, Sweet Home'. He goes back to the hall with Marcus, who talks about the smell of the villagers and is now back to his snobbish worst. He also tells Leo of the coming engagement of Marian and Trimingham.

Leo is still triumphant on Sunday, and he writes to his mother to beg that he may be allowed to stay another week. Ever curious, he notices in church that day that there is no memorial to the fifth viscount Trimingham. On questioning Trimingham, Leo finds that the fifth viscount was buried in France. He had fought a duel over his wife – the lady is never to blame, says Trimingham – but Leo draws parallels in his own mind between this past situation and the present triangle of Trimingham, Marian and Ted. In the afternoon Marcus goes to see

Nannie Robson at Marian's request. Marian meets Leo and asks him to take a letter to Ted. Leo is shocked, and at first refuses. His vision of Marian is shattered when, in a temper, she suggests that he wants money for his services. He snatches the letter and makes for the farmhouse; here he finds Ted preparing to clean his gun. Ted is kind to him, and teaches him the basics of shooting. In return Leo oils Ted's cricket bat and gives him Marian's letter. He asks Ted about 'spooning', but Ted is embarrassed. Leo responds by saying he will take no more messages unless Ted tells him everything, and Ted in return shouts at him and drives him away.

Leo now writes another letter to his mother saying that he is not enjoying himself, and begs her to send a telegram demanding his return home. Marian had signalled him to stay behind after tea, but he had ignored this. Later he learns from Trimingham that Marian is going to London the next day, and that Mrs Maudsley is ill. He also learns that Nannie Robson has, according to Marian, lost her memory. Leo meanwhile sets out for the outhouses, meeting Marcus on the way; their conversation is conducted mainly in French and pseudo-French. Marcus tells Leo that Mrs Maudsley is worried lest Marian should break off her engagement to Trimingham. Marcus also contradicts his sister's view of Nannie Robson's state of mind, but tells Leo the exciting news that Marian is going to buy him (Leo) a green bicycle for his birthday. This news is spoiled by Marcus's assertion that Marian thinks him (Leo) 'green', and Leo's response is to say that he knows where Marian is. As they approach the outhouses Leo sees that the deadly nightshade is now enormous; they hear voices, Leo recognizes Ted Burgess's, and cunningly gets Marcus away before he can discover anything. Leo considers retrieving the letter which he has written to his mother, but in the end he decides to let it go in the next collection.

Next morning it has gone, and so has Marian. Mrs Maudsley is still unwell. Leo spends Monday and Tuesday happily at the hall, looking forward to his mother's forthcoming telegram. He receives a letter from Ted who apologizes for his behaviour (when he lost his temper with Leo), and asks Leo to go to the farm on the Sunday. He says he will explain then what 'spooning' really is. Leo hopes to be back at home by that time. In the evening he asks Trimingham about Ted – more particularly, about the phrase 'getting your rag out' which had occurred in Ted's letter. Trimingham uses the same kind of slang, which Leo doesn't understand, telling him that Ted is a 'bit of a lady-killer'. Trimingham later reveals that he has had a word with Ted about going off to fight in the Boer War. As he leaves, Leo hears Mr Maudsley say that Ted has 'a woman up this way'. Leo thinks that he is speaking of the woman who comes in to clean for Ted.

No telegram arrives from Mrs Colston. On the Wednesday Leo decides that he will go to see Ted, to say goodbye. He assumes that he will be going on the Thursday, though he senses that the Maudsleys may wish him to remain there until he is given the green bicycle on the Friday at the tea party in his honour. When he sees Ted he tells him that he will be leaving, and asks Ted if he is going to fight in the war. Ted replies that it will depend on Marian; Leo, somewhat upset, offers to take a message for him; Ted's message is that Marian should meet him on Friday at 6.30 at the usual spot. At tea on Wednesday Leo receives a letter from his mother saying that she wants him to remain at Brandham Hall, and he wanders about in a confused state. The next morning Mrs Maudsley, recovered, takes her usual place at the breakfast table, but Marian talks to Leo afterwards. She is outraged to hear that Trimingham has suggested Ted joins the army; she intends to tell Trimingham that she will not marry him if Ted goes to fight. She cries when Leo asks her why she doesn't marry Ted, and he cries in return. Leo gives her Ted's message, but with an important falsification. He tells her that Ted will meet her at 6 o'clock not 6.30, thinking naïvely that if she has to wait it will end the relationship.

Leo believes that Ted has some magical power over Marian – a natural thought in view of his own interest in magic – and he determines to cast a spell which will break Ted's hold on Marian. That night he goes to the deadly nightshade, intending to strip off its leaves and branches to use in his spell. The plant seems to be moving towards him, and he becomes almost hysterical when it touches his face. He tears it up by the roots, falling backwards with its stump on him, and chanting in Latin that it must be destroyed. On the morning of his birthday, Friday 27 July, Leo is woken up; he is thirteen years old, rain is threatened, and he goes down to breakfast. He has letters from his mother and his aunt, as well as a tie from each. The tie from his aunt is, apparently, socially unacceptable on account of its colour and its made-up bow. Trimingham takes it and puts it on. Leo's embarrassment disappears. Afterwards the day is planned – a visit to see a castle (weather permitting) with the tea party coming later in the afternoon. Leo meanwhile has decided to wear his green suit.

The proposed trip is delayed because of the weather, but when Marian gets Leo outside she hurriedly gives him a letter for Ted. As she does so, her mother appears. Marian hastily explains the letter by saying that it is for Nannie Robson, arranging that she (Marian) will visit her that afternoon. Mrs Maudsley quickly leads Leo away into the gardens, and easily discovers from him that he has no idea where Nannie Robson lives. She interrogates him about the messages he has taken for Marian, but heavy rain interrupts this. At the birthday tea she treats Leo especially well. Marian is still not there and, thinking that it is too wet for her to make her way back from Nannie Robson's, Mr Maudsley sends the carriage for her. Meanwhile the cake is cut and the crackers are pulled. The butler enters to announce that Marian has not been to Nannie Robson's. Mrs Maudsley, despite her husband's disapproval, seizes Leo, determined that he shall lead her to where Marian is. Mrs Maudsley makes for the outhouses through a torrential downpour and, despite Leo's efforts to divert her, she forces him into a shed with her. They are confronted by the sight of Ted and Marian making love, and Mrs Maudsley dissolves into hysterics. This is virtually the end of the 'story', with the return to 1952 and Leo's remembering that, while he was still staying with the Maudsleys, he had heard that Ted Burgess had shot himself.

The Epilogue returns us, and Leo, to 1952. So moved by what he has remembered and in part analysed, Leo decides to go back to Brandham and piece together what happened after he had left the Maudsleys. Leo had turned away from personal relationships and concentrated on facts in his ensuing life. In his papers he has found Marian's last letter to Ted, still unopened. In this love-letter she says that she was going to give Leo the bicycle so that he could take her messages to Ted more conveniently. Leo's first call on arrival in Brandham is at the church. There he discovers that a tenth Viscount Trimingham had been born seven months after he (Leo) had left Brandham in 1900. A memorial exists to him, and Leo realizes that the eleventh viscount may still be living. He is, and in meeting him Leo realizes that he is Ted Burgess's grandson, now Lord Trimingham. Leo learns that Marian, a lonely and embittered old woman, is living in the cottage once inhabited by Nannie Robson. Marian is brooding on the fact that this grandson, feeling contaminated by the past, keeps away from her. She tells Leo what happened and shows, too, that she is living in a world of false ideas about her past and its effect on her family. She exercises her old influence on Leo when she asks him to take a message to her grandson. Leo is to tell him that Marian's love for Ted was right and noble and not shameful, and to urge upon the grandson the freedom to marry. Leo, with the past all around him, takes this last message to the hall. He is still the go-between.

The bald summary above is no substitute for the text of the novel, but it will enable you to check that text against the salient facts given in the summary. The next section of this Passnote will be devoted to a critical account of *The Go-Between*, with a chapter-by-chapter analysis. The student should follow this with the text. It is not possible to mention everything in a critical commentary, but always the reader should bear in mind characterization, style, setting, themes and plot. This will lead to a deeper appreciation of *The Go-Between* and its literary qualities after the first reading. That first reading should be undertaken at a fairly quick speed to catch the narrative flavour of action, events, character and the sheer *enjoyment* of the story.

An Account of the Plot

THE EPIGRAPH (the motto facing the Prologue)

Emily Brontë (1818–48) was the author of the novel *Wuthering Heights* (1847). The verse is related to the story here. The 'child of dust' could refer to Leo, dead in the sense of being 'killed' by his experiences at Brandham Hall. The rest of his life has not been fully lived. The 'strange conductors' were the various aspects of nature in that hot summer, the word 'strange' indicating the nature of his experience. In medieval times 'bowers' – places enclosed by trellis or foliage – were the traditional habitations of 'ladies' (like Marian) from which 'knights' (like Leo) were excluded. The other key word, 'daring', applies also to Leo, who is far from daring in ordinary life but 'dares' to test the unknown through his spells.

PROLOGUE, *pp. 7–21*

The flashback technique of *The Go-Between* is cleverly prepared for here. In returning to the *past* of things – the objects in the box – Leo as first-person narrator quickly returns to the *past* of people. His life between the ages of thirteen and sixty-five has been devoted to things rather than people. The opening claims the reader's attention: 'The past is a foreign country: they do things differently there' (p. 7). This is a reference to Leo's past, the difference he felt as an outsider at Brandham, and the behaviour of the adults in that past, 'foreign' to him now as an adult. The word 'foreign' is echoed in his description of the diary; it indicates that what it contains is foreign to him – he has deliberately shut it off. He puts himself into a spell, unlocks the diary, and unlocks that past which he fears because of what he feels it has done to him. The 'secret' flashes upon him, and he considers that what the diary contains has made him what he is. The signs of the zodiac represent his past interests. The innocence of the Virgin sign contrasts with the coming knowledge and the Virgin (Marian) who helps to change his life from innocence to unhappy experience. He recalls how these signs held the promise of the coming century and the promise of his own life, a 'Golden Age' (in classical mythology, the first and best age of mankind when all was happy, prosperous and innocent.

The young Leo hesitated in claiming the Lion as his symbol, for he proves to have few leonine qualities. There is a very interesting forecast of Leo's liking for Trimingham and Ted in his indecision over whether to choose the Archer or the Water-Carrier. The entries about school show the young Leo divided between concealment and showing off. A simile (comparison) describes his secrecy when he feels 'the intimate pleasure of brooding over the diary in secret, like a bird sitting on its eggs ...' (p. 12). The young Leo, subjected to bullying and being 'vanquished', casts his spells. He shows his learning on the one hand which contrasts with his simple, naïve schoolboy expression on the other, when he signs the curse BY ORDER   THE AVENGER. The older Leo admits he was a conformist, but the curse which (supposedly) brings down Jenkins and Strode makes him a respected outsider. He conforms to a dull adult life, but feels an outsider who has no sexual experience. Leo the boy has a conscience, and is 'secretly terrified' (p. 16) at what he thinks he has done through the curse. At the same time there is a delightfully humorous touch in the boys 'hoping for the worst' (p. 17), that is, the deaths of Jenkins and Strode. Leo is credited with not having brought this about by another curse.

Leo is an expert on 'black magic and code-making' (p. 17) before he goes to Brandham. The code-making becomes his obsession with facts as defence against life, and the boy recognizably becomes the man who has been beaten by life. It is one of Leo's traits always to be interested in words – note the 'ski' sequence here, again humorous – and part of his tragedy is that this intelligent little boy does not understand the commonplace slang words which convey adult responses and emotions – words like 'spooning', 'lady-killer' and 'got my rag out'.

When the adult Leo reaches 9 July as he flicks through the pages of the diary, he has virtually decided to try to de-code the past – and I choose the word 'de-code' deliberately, since he is trying to explain emotions not understood at the time. He also accepts the inevitability of what is going to happen through a simile 'like the loosening phlegm in an attack of bronchitis, waiting to come up' (p. 19). This image of illness reflects the nervous illness which Leo has suffered from as a man. There is something pathetic, even tragic, as the elderly Leo contemplates the diary and says 'My secret – the explanation of me – lay there' (p. 19).

Words like 'buried', 'embalmed', 'interment', 'exhumation', 'undertaker's art' (p. 19), show how determinedly Leo has buried the past. That past was a delusion, for the larger-than-life people of Brandham Hall were to him 'the incarnated glory of the twentieth century' (p. 19). He compares himself to the Icarus of classical mythology whose father made him wings, but 'You flew too near to the sun, and you were scorched' (p. 20). He links past and present in the schoolboy language of that past – 'You were vanquished, Colston, you were vanquished, and so was your century . . .' (p. 20). The Prologue ends with the single word LEO – the combination which unlocks the diary, and with it the past Leo who made the present Leo what he is.

CHAPTER 1, *pp. 22–31*

The movement from the present to the past is direct, immediate. Leo the adult has forgotten the boy Maudsley's Christian name, saying 'Perhaps it will come to me later' (p. 22). It does, as memory gradually opens up. There is a brief note on the snobbery current at the time – the name of Leo's home, Court Place, seems to have status to Marcus. A family consistency is established when Leo talks of his father whose hobbies 'enclosed him in himself' (p. 23) whereas his mother was 'attracted by the things of the world' (p. 23), aspects of character which are present in Leo the boy. The period atmosphere prior to the visit to Brandham Hall is seen in the mention of the landau (a four-wheeled horse-drawn carriage, p. 24). Marcus is neutral during the school episode until he sees that Leo is on the 'winning side' (p. 24). This shows him as an opportunist. Mrs Colston's response to Leo's status as a magician is neutral. She is a Christian lady, urging Leo to treat his former enemies well when they return to school. The outbreak of measles at school (p. 26) is necessary to the novel's plot: when Marcus succumbs to the illness later it frees Leo for his go-between activities. The early breaking up of school shows Leo very happy. His account of the farewell to the headmaster's family is even tinged with humour (the baby's 'acknowledgement' is 'comically regal' p. 27), and he is complacent since he is given the credit for the epidemic. He feels that his dreams for the twentieth century 'were coming true' (p. 28).

He looks back on the year 1899, when his father died. Leo himself had diphtheria, which made him fear the heat. This is important in view of the heatwave he is shortly to experience at Brandham Hall. Mrs Maudsley's letter to Mrs Colston is a mixture of kindness and snobbery – note the reference to 'the Season in the country', since it was then fashionable to spend that vacation in London. Leo assumes that the family has a personal interest in him. The dialogue between Leo and his mother is natural (p. 30), but again there is the stress on what may happen ('Promise me you'll let me know if you're not happy'). Leo does let her know, later, but to no good effect. The chapter ends with the natural interaction between Leo and his mother – she would really like to go to Brandham because of its social superiority. Leo has cold feet about going and urges her to tell the lie that he has measles. Mrs Colston wants him to go to church while he is there (Leo's later observation of the tablets in church is important). Leo, with delusions of his own magical power, considers that he will not need summer clothes. It is not going to be hot. He is wrong, and the coming heat is his enemy (his word) for life.

CHAPTER 2, *pp. 32–8*

The opening paragraph successfully conveys the dream-like effects of memory. Leo uses the diary to verify facts which he has forgotten, and the copying from the Norfolk directory shows the young Leo's attention to detail (it anticipates his later career, 'cataloguing other people's books' p. 20) and his snobbery – he is going to be a guest at a Georgian mansion which has art treasures. The interior is described factually by Leo. Mr Maudsley and his wife are seen at first as figures, the husband almost a caricature, but the impact of Mrs Maudsley remained with Leo throughout his life, for she is always in his dreams as an adult. And with adult hindsight he compares her to 'a portrait by Ingres or Goya' (see Glossary 1). The mixture is of boyish impressions and the adult Leo's knowledge. Already in this first account there is the strong sense that Mrs Maudsley is watching Marian. The number of guests conveys the social prestige of the house in the eyes of the young boy. The descriptions of clothes (and note the focus on this in the film of *The Go-Between*) reflect the period: e.g. the 'hourglass figures' of the girls. There are imaginative similes such as 'hats like windmills' (p. 35). There follows (after the first two days in which Leo is so overwhelmed that he hardly recognizes people as individuals) a description of Denys, assertive but easily punctured by his mother, and of Mr and Mrs Maudsley, the latter full of plans while her husband goes his 'gnome-like' way (p. 36). Perhaps most significant is Marcus's description of Marian as being 'very beautiful' (p. 36). Marian's beauty is soon to register with Leo. He describes her as being, like her mother, 'formidable' (p. 37). Young Leo was influenced by the signs of the zodiac, and the adult Leo, writing about these moments of his past, uses an image to describe the ladies 'who circled, planet-like, around the perimeter of my vision' (p. 37). Memory is selective, and Leo recalls 'floating impressions', the cedar, the crimson hammock (though these are not recorded in his diary) the coach-house, the smell of harness leather.

These sensations are climaxed by the diary entry about the 'Deadly Nightshade – Atropa Belladonna'. This is the central symbol of *The Go-Between*. A symbol is something that represents or stands for something else, and here the plant stands for Marian, for Mrs Maudsley, for sexual experience, for spells, for the poisoning of life. Here 'It looked the picture of evil and also the picture of health' (p. 38). Leo feels 'that if I didn't eat it, it would eat me' (p. 38). It fascinates Leo so much so that its Latin name ends the chapter with emphasis. The chapter is very visual. There is the period atmosphere, and there are the sensations and impressions of Leo, and his naturally inquiring mind. Notice too how, once certain memories return, other memories, apparently unconscious, follow them and almost complete the picture. I say 'almost' because Hartley's method through Leo, young and old, is to *gradually* complete the picture through experiences and discoveries which are made as the story unfolds.

CHAPTER 3, *pp. 39–46*

The temperature which marks the weather Leo didn't expect (remember that the heat is his enemy) makes a dramatic opening for the chapter. Marcus's report that his father 'likes to do the thermometer himself' (p. 39) points to Mr Maudsley being a 'fact' man (notice later how he gets runs, the facts of the game, in the cricket match). Mrs Maudsley is strongly ruled by emotions (hence her illness and her later hysteria). Leo becomes aware of his unsuitable clothes, and finds them recorded in a snapshot which reflects his self-consciousness at the time. Next, Marcus tells Leo what not to wear, for example, 'you mustn't come down to breakfast in your slippers' (p. 41), which carries a sting for the son of a bank manager who wore his at breakfast. For Leo the clothes–heat combination leads to what he calls 'a mild persecution' (p. 42). He therefore hatches a spell to bring down the temperature. It works temporarily, but the persecution, which shows people trying to take an interest in him, continues. Ever aware of words, he considers that 'It seemed doubly hard that a Norfolk jacket should be out of place in Norfolk' (p. 43). His sense of his social inferiority increases. Mrs Maudsley's voice 'like a current of cold air blowing towards me' (p. 43) makes Leo lie. He says that his mother forgot to pack his summer clothes. He is rescued by Marian. His humiliation changes to the hope that he and Marian will go to Norwich. We note Mrs Maudsley's attempts to dictate to Marian, the play on the word 'Hugh' and 'Who' which leads to passing confusion now (and later on) for Leo, Denys's inept interruption about Goodwood (see Glossary 1), and the first argument between Marian and her mother – 'it was like two steel threads crossing each other' (p. 45). Leo wonders jealously who this Hugh is, but happily finds that he has a 'shared secret' (p. 46) with Marian, who knows that he has no summer clothes.

CHAPTER 4, *pp. 47–59*

The story increases in pace and incident. Leo is made happy by Marian's attentions and taste – 'I came back not only feeling it was glorious to be me, but intimately satisfying to look like me' (p. 47). He has strong spiritual feelings about the cathedral after Marian has left him. His seeing her saying goodbye to someone is important to the plot, for later we learn that it was Ted Burgess. At tea Leo is aware of his 'apotheosis' (transformation) (p. 48). Then the play on the word 'green', at once a colour and also symbolic of innocence and naïveté, is used for the first time in the novel. Leo's romantic imagination seizes on the Robin Hood associations. He sees himself 'roaming the greenwood with Maid Marian' (p. 49). He feels Mrs Maudsley's intensity, being 'caught like a moth in the beam from her eye, that black searchlight' (p. 49). Her cross-questioning of Marian, seemingly casual, is probing.

Leo's new love for the heat reflects an innocent search for experience. He feels, 'if it would only get hotter and hotter there was a heart of heat I should attain to' (p. 50). He sees his new garments as being discarded one by one 'before the final release into nakedness' (p. 50). Mrs Maudsley won't allow Leo to go swimming without his mother's permission. We note that no mother's permission is considered when Leo begins to take messages. Mrs Maudsley sees Marian as an irresponsible influence in direct opposition to her own parental, family, social and moral responsibilities.

A fine phrase describes Leo's thoughts of the bathing party, 'this idea of surrendering oneself to an alien and potentially hostile element' (p. 52). Leo's conversation with Marcus keeps us well in mind of the wider background – the Boer War (See Glossary 1), Trimingham's wounds, Leo's father having been a pacifist. The foreground is that Mrs Maudsley wants Marian to marry Trimingham. Leo is already 'violently jealous' (p. 52) of him. Always we are aware of the continuing heat.

The first sight of Ted Burgess shows physical enjoyment without social convention (a foretaste of what is to come). There is the immediate contrast of Denys's silly comments and Marian's withdrawal to the period bathing machine (see Glossary 1). Denys reveals his hypocrisy when he says that Ted must not think that they are 'stuck-up' (p. 54), which is exactly what they are. When Ted crouches over the spike 'he looked as though he would be impaled' (p. 55). This is perhaps a subtle indication that if he gets out of his depth (socially) he will be hurt or worse, which is what happens when his affair with Marian is discovered. The period atmosphere is conveyed again through such details as the ladies' bathing dresses. Leo shows that he is becoming sexually aware when he notes that these dresses 'begin to cling to them [the girls] and take on the soft outlines of their bodies' (p. 56). When he sees Ted Burgess again, he retreats 'before that powerful body, which spoke to me of something I did not know' (p. 56). This is a fear of manhood and adult sexuality, Leo's reactions being reinforced by his seeing the now unaware Ted in near nakedness. For Leo Marian's appearance, with her two curves of hair, makes her 'the Virgin of the Zodiac' (p. 57). From now on he sees her in this way. Marian affects not to know anything of Ted (she is cunning and cautious). Leo makes a long speech in offering her his bathing suit. Sexual innocence and courteous conduct are seen in this action. He spreads her hair – 'A labour of love it truly was, the first I had ever done' (p. 58). The language of the adult Leo explains the reactions of the boy Leo, and is much more directly sexual. 'My thoughts enveloped her, they entered into her: I was the bathing-suit on which her hair was spread; I was her drying hair ...' (p. 59).

CHAPTER 5, *pp. 60–66*

Leo gets used to the daily family prayers and rituals. The boy Leo shoots the rapids of the stairs (the language of his imagination). He considers a spell against Trimingham, but when he sees the latter – note the detail of the description which conveys the horror of the wound – he finds that he is thinking about why the family is nice to Trimingham. Again Leo's naïveté is revealed, even to his believing that Marian's opening her blue eyes at Trimingham is because she is sorry for him. There is more social instruction from Marcus – it is correct to eat porridge while walking about if you are male. Marcus himself is laid low with measles. This leads to an exchange of period slang ('trickle along', 'hard cheese') and some more snobbery from Marcus, who holds that the annual cricket match 'helps to keep them [the villagers] quiet' (p. 63). The ball in honour of Marian's and Trimingham's engagement is to be held on 28 July. There is some comic action as Leo holds his breath in order to avoid catching Marcus's germs. When he joins the procession to church a humorous note enters his account, and sometimes he laughs at himself ('Composing my features into pious lines' p. 64). Note Mrs Maudsley's generous action in giving Leo a shilling for the collection (she has sensed that he has little money, and probably imagines what his family circumstances are like). Marian's self-absorbed state is shown by her forgetting what Leo had told her about his family, while Leo's ignorance of girls is shown in his asking her about her hair: 'Does it only come down by accident?' (p. 65). Marian does not encourage Trimingham on the walk.

CHAPTER 6, *pp. 67–75*

Leo superstitiously counts the Psalms for the day, with their verses. His study of the Trimingham tablets finds him, typically, asking questions and relating past history to present life. The church gives him a sense of awe, but the religion, the glory 'began to identify itself with the Zodiac, my favourite religion' (p. 68). Leo's consciousness is active, and he takes out his watch to bet with himself how long the Litany will last. His actions are the actions of a natural if somewhat precocious boy with an inquiring and restless mind, superstitious, believing he will become ill if certain rituals are not followed. He even, in his inner independence, begins to parody (mock) the biblical terms he is hearing ('How would it profit a man if he got into a tight place . . . ?' pp. 69–70). He feels (and he doesn't know how soon it is to happen), 'I longed, I thought, to be tested' (p. 70). Everything confirms his ideas that Triminghams and Maudsleys are 'a race apart, super-adults' (p. 70). Leo, his mind often thinking about the zodiac, misses what is obvious with monotonous regularity. As he admits himself, 'Two and two never made four for me, if I could make them five' (p. 71). His love for Marian is expressed in the slang of the day ('ripping', 'spifflicating', p. 72) and, most important, he casts *himself* as go-between by saying 'I could run errands for her – you know, carry things and take messages' (p. 72). The confusion over the pronunciation of 'Hugh' and 'who' embarrasses Leo, but perhaps Marian is being deliberately awkward.

Leo reminds Hugh that he is a guest in his own house. He is sensitive when he goes to his new room. It is a cell (almost an anticipation of his adult monastic existence), but he feels intuitively, 'I was cast for a new role' (p. 75). He is, and in wearing the new clothes he becomes 'a Robin Hood in Lincoln green' (p. 75) setting off to serve Maid Marian. The alert reader will be aware of the other meaning of the word 'green'.

CHAPTER 7, *pp. 76–89*

Leo feels a 'convert' to the heat, and speaks of 'the climate of my emotions' (p. 76), also talking about the 'small change of experience' and of wanting 'to deal in larger sums' (p. 76). These metaphors (comparisons without using 'like' or 'as') show how vividly Hartley writes. Leo feels too that 'my old life was a discarded husk' (p. 77). There is a powerful paragraph on the physical effects of the heat, which has its own smell and, for Leo, its own spell. The changed sounds and the changed sense of touch, the changed senses, make Leo 'another person' (p. 77). He continues to see the people at Brandham in terms of zodiac signs but, wishing to be alone, eventually comes to the farm. He also becomes a natural boy again by sliding down the straw-stack, despite a last-minute fear. It is an important action, this innocent sliding symbolic of the moral slide (secrecy, deception) to come. There is a vivid suddenness about Leo hurting his knee and in the description and reaction of Ted Burgess, particularly when he learns that Leo is from the hall. There is also a rough kindness in Ted which is not just an acknowledgement of what Leo calls 'hierarchical principles' (p. 80). Leo's own snobbery makes him note Ted's 'mean abode' (p. 80). The dialogue between Ted and Leo is natural. Leo, conscious of a debt to Ted for his kindness in bandaging the knee, asks the question which leads to his becoming the go-between – 'Is there anything I can do for you?' (p. 81). Ted is physically impressive ('He always seemed to speak with his whole body' p. 82) and his introduction of Leo to the horses forces us to think of their names – Briton is a patriotic choice and reminds us we are in a time of war. Smiler will be in foal later as a result of 'spooning' – while Wild Oats is what Ted and Marian are sowing. Leo is ignorant of what it means. Once more this word-conscious little boy is defeated by the commonplace of slang. Ted's questioning, and a certain physical threat about him, lead Leo to reveal just what Ted wants to know – 'So you are on your own, like' (p. 83). He also draws Leo out, and the boy shows off (notice that he twice mentions 'Viscount Trimingham'). He refers to himself as Marian's 'sweetheart' (p. 84), though acknowledging that the word is Denys's. Ted is aware of the class division between himself and Marian – 'I'm a kind of friend of hers, but not the sort she goes about with' (p. 85). Leo admits that he is 'a born intriguer' (p. 86). Ted is sensitive enough to understand that there *is* something different about Leo, as if he feels that Leo is a victim or sufferer, when he says 'Be kind to yourself' (p. 87). Marian's real nature is revealed, though Leo is ignorant of it, when he says that 'her face had the hooded, hawk-like look it sometimes wore' (p. 88). Romantically, sentimentally, she keeps Ted's handkerchief, and her response to his letter is so emotional that when she has hidden it she can't remember having bandaged Leo's leg, or even that Marcus is ill in bed. This shows her emotional nature. She is obviously moved by what Ted has written.

CHAPTER 8, *pp. 90–100*

Leo notices that Lord Trimingham's presence in the house has made a difference. He sees that Mrs Maudsley pays much attention to Trimingham, though Leo is ignorant at this stage of the marriage to come between Marian and Trimingham. The period flavour is conveyed by the picnics (even down to the detail of the lemonade bottle 'with a glass marble for a stopper' p. 90). Named Mercury by one of his gods (Trimingham), Leo is very happy. Then he awakes from sleep to hear Marian plotting that he should be alone (note her cunning), and Mrs Maudsley regretting that there are thirteen of them (she is superstitious, like Leo). Leo continues to idealize and idolize Trimingham ('His gaiety had a background of the hospital and the battlefield' p. 92). He thinks of his 'gods' as speaking a 'foreign' language, 'star-talk' (p. 92). We note the echo in 'foreign' of the opening sentence of the novel – so much of what Leo hears is foreign to him. He enjoys the period drive through the countryside, though he notices the children 'scrabbling on the ground for the pennies which the coachman nonchalantly threw them' (p. 93). The coachman refers to Ted Burgess as 'a bit of a lad' (p. 93), which Leo does not understand. There is a vivid description of the ascent and descent of the carriages on the hills, and more period reference in the detail of what Lord Trimingham is wearing. Leo's reception of his mother's letter, with everything at home seeming small, shows how far he has travelled in his dream at Brandham, for 'here I was a planet' (p. 95). He writes an answer, but he knows that he is 'a touch condescending' (p. 95) as he tells his mother of all that has been happening and what is still to come. Leo notes the record temperature and thinks of himself as the mercury within. It is a happy, uncomplicated feeling, and he thinks of 'new heights', 'unexplored altitudes', 'the mountain on which my experience would be won' (p. 96). He sees the peaks as 'the cricket match, my birthday party, and the ball' (p. 96). Trimingham uses more colloquialisms which Leo does not understand, like 'to sneak past in dead ground' (the latter a military phrase meaning ground which is hidden below what can be seen) and, more significantly, Trimingham's reference to Marian, 'I believe you have her in your pocket' (p. 97). This anticipates Leo putting Marian's final note to Ted in his pocket, Mrs Maudsley seeing this, and later reprimanding him for having his hands in his pockets. Marian and Leo meet near the outhouse. She has been with Ted (though Leo does not suspect this), and the confusion over 'Hugh' and 'who' reflects both Leo's and Marian's confusion at the sudden meeting. Leo does notice that Marian is 'breathing rather quickly' (p. 98), and he is aware that she is 'guiding the conversation, and half clairvoyantly I followed her lead' (p. 99). She nearly gives herself away over Ted. Her decision to join the croquet players after her snappy refusal to do so shows that Marian knows she has acted impetuously.

CHAPTER 9, *pp. 101–10*

Leo is now fully launched as messenger. He describes Ted as 'a sheaf the reaper had forgotten' (p. 101). When he hands the letter to him 'a long smear of blood appeared on the envelope' (p. 102). Leo is at first horrified, though he afterwards accepts it 'as part of a man's life into which I should one day be initiated' (p. 102). Ted has just killed something. The blood perhaps symbolizes the wounding of Leo later, perhaps the spilling of the virgin's blood in the final glimpse which Leo has of Ted and Marian making love, and more certainly, the spilling of Ted's own blood when he commits suicide. Leo humorously refers to Mrs Maudsley's 'after breakfast orderly-room' (someone else's phrase) (p. 102), an echo of the military language he associates with Trimingham. Leo's continuing infatuation with Marian is stressed, but he is also thinking about the messages (a bank manager's son, he feels 'like a bank-messenger' p. 103). Leo welcomes the return downstairs of Marcus, but he finds his role as messenger cramped. He knows that Marcus's games – more period reference – are likely to be concerned with contemporary Boer or English military leaders. In any case Marcus could not be brought to mix with Ted Burgess. Leo has a code of morality (although he knows he is a deceiver) which makes him want to keep up his relationship with Marcus. Leo is now inwardly worried, loath to give up serving Marian, loath to abandon his fantasy of being Robin Hood to her Maid Marian. There is a dramatic incident when Trimingham interrupts Marian giving Leo a note, but Hugh (who is later described by the old Marian as 'true as steel' p. 277), suspects nothing.

The conversation between Leo and Marcus, with its private language, is suggestive, for Marcus uses the word 'spooning' and Leo says that he is quite certain that Marian doesn't spoon (p. 107). His discovery that Marian's letter is unsealed puts Leo in a quandary, and he refers to the schoolboy code of not reading sealed letters but being allowed to look at those which are unsealed. Leo, as ever, justifies what he does by reference to fact (unsealed) rather than intention (whether or not she meant to seal it). But Marian is outside the code, 'dividing my thoughts against themselves' (p. 109). Leo gives in, and the chapter ends on a sad and dramatic note with Leo reading Marian's loving words to Ted.

CHAPTER 10, *pp. 111–19*

The reference to Adam and Eve which opens the chapter immediately suggests a loss of innocence. Leo is disillusioned. Half-ignorant, prejudiced, somewhat prudish by nature, Leo suffers the pangs of misguided love. In his mind Marian comes down from the zodiac to earth. The narrowness of his education has made him associate love with the sordid jokes of the seaside picture-postcards. He thinks to protect Marian, sealing the letter 'to cover her shame' (p. 112). Gradually Leo accepts the idea of Marian 'spooning', but when he meets Ted he has made his decision, little realizing that this is going to bring more hurt upon himself. Leo is rather pleased that Ted is 'chap-fallen' (p. 113), but Ted knows that Leo wants Marian's friendship. The dialogue is uneven because of Ted's dominance, and Leo is 'half hypnotized' (p. 114) by him. Ted produces his trump card with superb economy, referring to Marian crying. He knows that Leo is easily moved and that this is the way to move him deeply. Leo once more fails to understand slang. Smiler is 'in the family way' (p. 115) says Ted, but although Leo pretends to understand he doesn't. As he says, 'The facts of life were a mystery to me' (p. 115). The dialogue about spooning is a great embarrassment to Ted. Leo, the bookish boy, asks the questions which will lead to the facts but Ted, conscious of the difficulty of being blunt to the innocent, is forced into using the unsuitable term 'lover-like' (p. 117), which proves even more bewildering to Leo. Leo's question about spooning leading to a baby gets a reaction from Ted, for 'His ruddy face went mottled' (p. 117). (Ted's spooning with Marian is later to result in a baby whom Ted does not live to see, but whom Trimingham nobly accepts as his own.) Ted plays for time with Leo. He promises to tell him about spooning if Leo will continue to be 'our postman' (p. 118) and Leo, when he agrees, realizes that in the relationship of Marian and Ted there is 'a suggestion of beauty and mystery' (p. 118).

CHAPTER 11, *pp. 120–32*

Denys and Trimingham at breakfast on Saturday morning are talking in clichés about the forthcoming cricket match and the ability of Ted Burgess, with Trimingham correctly prophesying how they will get him out. There is mockery of Mrs Maudsley's affected pronunciation ('duke' for 'duck'). The 'conclave' is a parody or mockery of the serious way the English take their cricket, and the sense of correct behaviour is seen in the choice of the pantry boy rather than Leo to play in the game. The dialogue is suggestive. Trimingham's request that Marian sing 'Home, Sweet Home' implies that it is her sweet home that she is marrying for. Leo, by saying that he likes Trimingham, moves Marian to a small reflex action – she pricks her finger on a rose thorn and thrusts the flowers into their vases in a 'vindictive way' (p. 123). Just as Ted got around Leo, so Marian now urges him to stay longer at Brandham Hall. She sees that she can easily use him. She is still vindictive towards Trimingham, saying that she will sing his request if he will sing 'She Wore a Wreath of Roses'. Leo is upset to find that Trimingham doesn't sing, and that he is wounded by Marian's reply. Leo tries to con Trimingham into thinking that the reply was a joke. The older Leo, aware of what later happens, observes sympathetically, 'It might have been better if I had left him with his original impression' (p. 125). Leo himself tells Marian that Trimingham laughed. Delighted with his lie, he observes that 'I was beginning to fancy myself as an editor as well as a messenger' (p. 126). Marcus puts Leo right with regard to correct cricket wear. On the way to the match Leo registers the fact that 'class distinctions melted away' (p. 127). He associates the villagers with the Boers who were fighting the British with little equipment but strong courage. Leo and Ted are mutually embarrassed by being formally introduced to each other. Trimingham makes a remark which is unconsciously near the truth when he says 'But you should make him run errands for you, Burgess, he's a nailer at that' (p. 128).

Leo next describes the 'accessories' which make the match an occasion and give it importance. Boyishly, he confesses his loyalty: 'I felt that the honour of the Hall was at stake' (p. 129). The honour of the hall – Marian's affair with Ted – is at stake in a way that Leo doesn't understand. Leo admits his own snobbery as he watches. He looks at Lord Trimingham with 'the sense of consequence his condescension gave me' (p. 129). Denys shows off by mentioning the famous contemporary cricketer R. E. Foster. Trimingham's batting symbolizes Trimingham in life – he scores only a few runs. Marian applauds as Trimingham comes in, to show that there is nothing wrong between herself and Hugh, and perhaps to kill any suspicions her mother may have of her. Mr Maudsley's innings, like Ted's later, is one of the high points of the match, and for a different reason. He plods but is successful, he shows a fitting sense of responsibility, he does not make mistakes;

Ted, when he bats, is the very reverse – dashing, powerful, risky, entertaining, out. The class contrast between them is implicit. As Leo puts it, Mr Maudsley represents the brain against brawn in his treatment of the village bowling. His authority is nowhere better seen than in the farcical but brief partnership with the silly Denys, who is finally – and perhaps deliberately – run out by his father.

CHAPTER 12, *pp. 133–40*

Leo's judgement is once more shown to be at fault, for he feels that the villagers will lose as their batsmen are got out. Leo notices a cloud, which is vividly, and somewhat ominously, described. Ted Burgess's batting brings Leo down to earth. Note the speed of the narration – Ted nearly out, Ted hitting 'a really glorious six' (p. 134), the emphasis on luck, the passing contrast with Mr Maudsley's innings; in a superb comparison, the older Leo sees the innings of each of them as 'the struggle between order and lawlessness, between obedience to tradition and defiance of it, between social stability and revolution' (p. 135).

Leo speaks to Marian, and finds that she is too excited, too moved to speak. When the fielder is injured, the imaginative Leo even thinks that he may be wounded for life, and Ted sent to prison as a result. These reactions spring from the excitement of Ted's innings and the question of which side will win. We feel that Trimingham's repeated 'We've got to get him out' (p. 137) means more than he says: that Ted must be defeated for all eyes to see, that in a sense battle has been joined and Marian is the reward. Leo, ever superstitious, manages to stand in a 'fairy ring' (p. 137). The tension is broken by the mistake on the scoreboard, yet when play resumes there is increased tension because the villagers now need only eight runs to win. Leo is confused now in his loyalties, but when Ted hits a four he decides that he wants the village to win. Yet it is his brilliant catch which sees to it that the hall wins. He feels regret in his elation; the regret being 'sharp as a sword-thrust' (p. 139). He does not know what to say to Ted. The latter is generous in defeat, admitting 'I . . . never thought I'd be caught out by our postman' (p. 140). The 'postman' is later to be hurried to the spot where Ted and Marian are making love and forced to be responsible for catching them both out. It is significant that Marian does not look up as Ted enters the pavilion; presumably, she is still too moved to trust herself to do so.

CHAPTER 13, *pp. 141–52*

Leo notes the atmosphere – he calls it 'matiness' (p. 141) – of supper in the village hall. We note that there is a determined attempt to break the class barriers for this one night of the year. Once again Leo misjudges the ability of Mr Maudsley, whose dry jokes are successful. He mentions by name everybody who played. Leo is compared to David 'who slew the Goliath of Black Farm' (p. 142). Marian's decision to play the piano may be a deliberate act of rebellion, since she knows that Ted sings and that Trimingham can't. She and Ted will be together in everyone's view. Leo continues to be romantically entranced by Marian. Ted is embarrassed, and there is comedy in his announcing 'Take a Pair of Sparkling Eyes' when he doesn't want to take anything. The reality of the scene is well conveyed, with genuine audience response both collective and individual. Ted's modesty – it is probably embarrassment – is stressed, but the Balfe song has words which express love and relate to the situation of the lovers, Ted and Marian. Despite this, Leo did not 'connect such manifestations with the phenomenon called spooning' (p. 145). There is a significant audience comment as Ted and Marian take their bows – 'If it wasn't for the difference, what a handsome pair they'd make' (p. 145).

Leo the boy, asked to sing, has the hindsight of the older Leo to describe his reactions. He calls it 'the second time I was called upon to exchange the immunities of childhood for the responsibilities of the grown-up world' (p. 146). Leo enjoys the singing because it is service to Marian – 'She was my Land of Song' (p. 147) – but he also uses Christian language when he is summoned to sing: 'It was like a death but with a resurrection in prospect' (p. 146). During the song he refers to 'a whole series of deaths which I should die for her. Each was quite painless, of course: a crown without a cross' (p. 147). This suggests that Leo rather enjoys being a martyr, a victim (though he has no idea of the suffering which is to come. When reality hits him, he has a breakdown.) Note Leo's wish for 'something worse than death' and that he is singing a woman's song, the heroine being threatened 'with something worse than death' (p. 148), that is, disgrace. Ted's generosity is evident once more – his is the genuine tribute to Leo's singing – and there is Leo's own response and thoughts about Marian's singing 'Home, Sweet Home'.

There is some anti-climax after the concert in the schoolboy expressions into which Marcus and Leo naturally slip, but there is considerable humour too in the mutual baiting of two intelligent and even witty boys. Marcus shows his snobbery about the villagers, and hints at his mother's suspicions about Ted and Marian. He is also jealous of Leo. When he accuses Leo of looking so *pi* (pious) we realize that Marcus, with all his knowledge of convention and social propriety, lacks Leo's innocence. The chapter ends with the news that Marian's engagement to Trimingham will be announced after the ball, and Leo expresses his gladness. Marcus's announcement can only, however, lead to more complications of feeling in Leo.

CHAPTER 14, *pp. 153–62*

Leo is triumphant on the Sunday morning. He feels that he belongs to the 'celestial world. I was one with my dream life' (p. 153). He defines his triumph by reference to Jacob's ladder (which enabled one to reach blissful heights) but again makes a passing mention of Icarus. Leo is coming closer and closer to scorching. Although he approves of the Trimingham–Marian match, his feelings for Ted Burgess are strong, and he, perhaps half-consciously, uses a phrase which is from his own practice and superstition – 'his mere physical presence cast a spell on me' (p. 154). The phrase is significant because, just as a spell is a mystery, so Ted represents the mystery of sex for Leo. He acknowledges his jealousy of Ted but, despite his class awareness, says that he would like to be like Ted when he grows up. Leo feels that the relationship that he has with Ted is now harmonious, mainly, we suspect, because of Leo's pride in his own triumph. Leo begins to have an inflated opinion of himself (particularly after the servant's praise) and his opinions stiffen – he feels that the engaged Marian can have no more messages for him, and thinks of happiness in simple terms. The delusion is so strong that the letter he writes to his mother shows complacency and social conceit. Superstition continues to rule, but a count of the Psalms ('seven below the danger-line' p. 157) sustains his happy mood, and another contemplation of the Trimingham tablets, eventually to have the addition of Marian's name, convinces him that the race of Triminghams is 'immortal' (p. 157). The story of the fifth viscount, the death in the duel, Leo's probing questions about whether he would have minded 'if he hadn't been married to her but just engaged?' (p. 161), all this dialogue has the Marian–Trimingham–Ted triangle in mind. The Frenchman is good-looking and a good shot, like Ted. Leo has a craving for sensation, and in a moment of rare humour sees men fighting over 'a carpet of prostrate women' (p. 162). The chapter ends with Hugh's tolerance of the enemy (the Boer). Perhaps the suggestion is his tolerance also of Marian's 'human frailty'.

CHAPTER 15, *pp. 163–77*

Leo takes to heart Trimingham's statement that nothing is ever a lady's fault. Marcus's news that he is going to visit Nannie Robson sets the final phase of the plot in motion, and his abhorrence of smells is the opposite of Leo's fascination with the rubbish heap. Leo sees Marian as ministering to the poor, but his dream is interrupted by the real Marian asking him to take a letter to Ted. The effect is immediate: 'The scaffolding of my life seemed to collapse: I was dumbfounded' (p. 165). With Trimingham's story of the duel in mind, Leo fears the consequences, but his mention of 'Hugh' is once again misunderstood by Marian, who thinks he means her – 'you'. When she realizes what he does mean her mood changes to one of anger. She is like her mother in immediate reaction and Leo feels 'her nose hawk-like, her body curved to pounce' (p. 166). Her temper hurts Leo immediately, and her suggestion that he wants paying is an additional wound. When he runs from her Leo still does not understand, for the word 'Shylock' is beyond him. She has lifted him to achievement, but now she has withdrawn all from him 'like an enchantress' (p. 168). At the same time he sees clearly the nature of his delusion, that Marian has in reality done everything for him from 'an ulterior motive' (p. 168). He pauses, after his tears, by the pool, which (note the superb detail of the description) becomes the symbol of his defeat, the destruction of his dream. He goes over all Marian's actions, for Leo is very thorough, and convinces himself that all of them have served her ends. Still Trimingham's phrase echoes through his mind as he kicks a stone, though he also feels as though he is being watched by another part of himself as he goes on, concluding: 'Perhaps it was the part of me that would not take the letter' (p. 170). Again he is overcome by tears, but when he does enter the kitchen he finds Ted sitting with a gun. What he sees is of direct importance, for it is a visual anticipation, here in the innocent pose, of Ted's coming suicide. Ted knows how to win over the upset Leo, mentioning the catch, which makes Leo feel more like his normal self. The shooting of the bird is also calculated to get Leo out of his mood, and Leo recognizes this, observing that 'The deed of blood had somehow sealed a covenant between us' (p. 172). Proudly holding the gun Leo, again innocently, points it straight at Ted. Reprimanded by Ted, he feels 'almost a murderer' (p. 173). The oiling of the bat which to Leo seems like 'the bow of Ulysses' (See Glossary 1) (p. 173) is symbolic of Leo's wish to serve Ted – even, in a way, to make up for the catch. The little boy asks the innocent question 'do you have a woman every day?', unaware of the meaning of the phrase. For a fleeting moment Ted looks at him. Ted knows that it is Marian who has hurt the boy, tries to make amends, then talks of Leo's singing as a way of flattering him. Leo obstinately pursues his own point, the payment he wants being the promised definition of 'spooning'. Ted refuses, showing how caring he is when he says 'It might spoil it for you' (p. 176). Life has just been spoiled for Leo by Marian. (When he sees the act of 'spooning' his future life is spoiled for him as well.) The tension mounts as Ted tries to tell Leo but can't, using Leo's 'best' experiences as substitutes for direct definition. Leo traps him, Ted is frustrated and angered but 'Armoured by his nakedness, he took a step towards me' (p. 177). Once more a chapter has ended on a high note of drama and expectation.

CHAPTER 16, *pp. 178–84*

The schoolboyish address gives way to the urgent plea: a complete contrast with the previous letter, it reflects Leo's new sense of insecurity. His fears are misguided – he sees Trimingham as the victim of Ted's anger, but Trimingham is strong while Ted, physically strong, is not so strong emotionally. Leo finds other excuses for being summoned home, playing on his mother's concern for his health and on her ideas of Rather Wrong and Very Wrong. Leo describes how he ran from Ted, the latter's anger adding to his emotional suffering. Marian at tea is in a happy mood (this almost certainly means that she is preparing something or covering up). Leo imagines the future of Marian and Trimingham, believing that after their marriage she will be 'in full view, and he [Trimingham] half in shadow' (p. 181). This anticipates the fact that she is 'in full view' after Ted's death when she has borne his son, while Trimingham is 'half in shadow' – as well as being scarred – by what she has done. There is some mockery in Leo's account of the over-plentiful teas at Brandham Hall and 'the decorous sounds we all made eating and drinking' (p. 181). Leo, not responding to Marian's signal, continues naïvely to believe that if he departs the affair between Marian and Ted will finish. Two things affect Leo now – the fact that his letter will not go until the next day and Trimingham's asking him to resume his role of go-between by finding Marian. Leo's remembering that Marian is at Nannie Robson's causes Trimingham to observe that Marian has said that Nannie Robson is losing her memory. The close of the chapter once more arouses expectation. Mrs Maudsley's illness – has she discovered exactly what is going on, or does she *fear* that something is going on? – reflects the disease of deception which is being practised.

CHAPTER 17, *pp. 185–95*

There is a delightful comic interchange in slang, French and pseudo-French, between Marcus and Leo which takes the edge off the mounting tension. The boys are balanced 'between affection and falling out' (p. 185). The visit to the outhouses reveals Leo's fear of the deadly nightshade. On several occasions he has turned back out of fear. He says that the only person he has seen near the outhouses is Marian. Marcus reveals that his mother is neurotic and has been made ill because of the 'strain' over whether Marian will stick to her engagement (despite the fun, the tension begins to rise again at this). Leo panics as he ponders on how much Mrs Maudsley knows, indeed how much Marcus knows, and whether they are in league together. He is also worried that Marian has rarely seen Nannie Robson who is not, according to Marcus, losing her memory. His mood becomes happier when he learns that Marian has gone to buy him a present. Leo is so excited that he forgets to fear Marian's presents 'and their Danaan implication' (p. 188) (See Glossary 1). Marcus is equally delighted to be able to point out that the colour of the bicycle is to be green. Leo is deeply hurt that Marian had said of him that it was his 'true colour' (p. 190).

In his reaction he boasts that he knows where Marian is at that moment, a dangerous boast if Marcus is indeed his mother's spy. This appears likely from the quick way in which Marcus takes up Leo's remark. Fortunately Leo responds in French to counter Marcus's 'little boys' taunt. Leo knows that Marcus is a tell-tale and this makes him uneasy. He is fascinated by the appearance of the deadly nightshade, which has grown so much that it almost gives the effect of moving. The detailed description of it makes it into the central symbol of the novel, beautiful, fascinating, demanding, like Marian. Mysteriously, 'It exhibited all the stages of its development at once. It was young, middle-aged, and old at the same time' (p. 192). These represent life experience which, of course, the young Leo does not possess. Yet he is very close to it, for he hears Ted Burgess's voice. What he doesn't realize is that Ted is urging, pleading with Marian to let him make love to her. There is a strong sense in the writing of what-might-have-been there and then if the lovers had been discovered. Leo ensures that they are not discovered – he is at the moment terrified of seeing 'spooning', particularly between Ted and Marian – by the simple use of the word 'ennuyeux' (boring) as the only means of getting Marcus away. We feel that Marcus will tell his mother about this, though he doesn't know the actual truth, since Marian's engagement is uppermost in their minds. Leo now wrestles with the idea of accepting the bicycle. He goes somewhat dramatically to the letter box, sees that his letter is there, takes it out but puts it back. He has rejected the bicycle in his mind.

CHAPTER 18, *pp. 196–207*

Leo thinks about the absence of Marian and Mrs Maudsley, particularly
the latter who, although she has been kind to him, makes him apprehens-
ive too. Leo feels that he will soon be out of Brandham, but this is
another of his delusions. He fails to understand the grown-up reaction,
this time to his letter. The fact that the letter remains unanswered for
so long, and that there is no telegram, increases tension. Leo considers
Marian's influence on him. Her vision of him is what is important, so
that his image of himself – 'The portrait wouldn't come to life unless
she held the mirror' – is made all the more poignant when he adds 'And
now the mirror was cracked' (p. 197). The older Leo notices a reduction
in tension with Marian's departure. Even Denys feels the freedom of
his mother's absence. Marcus refers to his mother and Marian as the
'awe-inspirers' (p. 199) (he thinks he is being very clever and naughty
by punning 'awe' and 'whore', but this is a foreign language to Leo).
Leo imagines Marian in London buying the bicycle, begins to long for
his mother's letter, and then unexpectedly receives a letter from Ted.
Despite the directness and apparent sincerity of the letter, Leo is still
suspicious. He is able to put this letter aside because he thinks he will
shortly be well away from Brandham. Once again the slang phrase in
the letter ('got my rag out' p. 202) bewilders Leo, but in seeking out
Trimingham to find the meaning of it, he is faced with a number of
slang or colloquial expressions which, as I said earlier, are a foreign
language to him. The men going to the smoking-room, like the elaborate
tinkling at tea, conveys period atmosphere. Trimingham explains the
difficult phrase for Leo, but uses an even more bewildering term in
'lady-killer' (p. 204). The pictures also bother Leo; they represent low-
life gambling and sex and he is disgusted, observing 'They got something
out of being their naked selves' (p. 205). Trimingham cares for Leo's
innocence, and turns the subject away from the pictures. Ted may be
persuaded to join up. There is humour too, for Leo knows that Ted has
a woman (to do his cleaning) and interprets Mr Maudsley's 'They say
he's got a woman up this way' (p. 207) as a reference to that.

CHAPTER 19, *pp. 208–17*

Marcus tells Leo about the ball, and obviously enjoys showing off. Leo
is still convinced that he won't be there to take part in it but gets on
well with Marcus at this time. Next Marcus talks about Leo's birthday
party, when Marian is going to make a splendid entrance – in tights or
bloomers – a picture which excites Leo. The sexual nature of this is
obvious, but not to Leo. If Marian does wear tights she will be behaving
unconventionally. The weather, which has influenced Leo so much, is
'Set Fair' (p. 211), but there is no telegram for him. On Wednesday
Leo reads *Punch*, and we notice the period reference of the jokes. Leo's
fear – about 'a bomb that would explode at tea-time' (p. 213) – is slightly
inaccurate, since the crisis in Leo's life occurs on his birthday. Leo tells
a lie in order to get rid of Marcus – he says Ted is going to give him a
swimming lesson – but when he faces Ted he sees him as 'the husk of
the man he had been' (p. 215). The reader is left to consider whether
this is because of Marian's engagement or because he has been urged
to enlist. Leo offers to take a last message. One part of him is sincerely
'grieved' (p. 217) at parting from Ted, and we are moved when he asks
Ted to call him 'postman' for what is the last time. But there is another
side to Leo – for, as we later see, he alters the time in the message in an
attempt to break the relationship. There is one ominous description –
'the rope was draped like a halter round my neck' (p. 217). It is a
threatening death image and, in delivering the message, Leo is ensuring
the death of the relationship between Marian and Ted and the death of
Ted (although he does not know this).

CHAPTER 20, *pp. 218–29*

Mrs Colston's conventional letter, with its cautious tone, its refusal to
act in haste, ensures that Leo will have to see out the climax. There is
light humour in her taxing Leo with his spelling 'grate' for 'great'. We
can't help feeling that she is trying, without any understanding, to do
the right thing; that she is thinking of herself, that if Leo leaves
Brandham it will reflect on him but also on her because of the way she
has brought him up. There are commonplaces like 'We can't expect to

be happy *all* the time, can we?' (p. 220) and the unconsciously ironic postscript 'All this will be an *experience* for you, my darling' (p. 220). The coming experience is to change Leo's life. He feels betrayed both by Marian and his own mother, though he realizes that his mother does not really know what she is doing. Leo, determined to change the situation, decides to falsify the time of the meeting between Marian and Ted.

There is a fine description of the return of Mrs Maudsley to the breakfast table – 'her glance still had its special quality of not travelling but arriving' (p. 222). Marian monopolizes Leo after breakfast, and reveals that she has been unhappy away from Brandham. Marian's reference to the hardness of her bed – she means of course her lot in life – is misunderstood by Leo, who thinks that she has actually slept on the ground. There is further confusion over the word 'Hugh', the usual misunderstanding between Marian and Leo. Leo drops his bombshell that Ted is going to the war. Once again he has blundered in the adult world, forgetting that Marian could not know that Trimingham had seen Ted after she had gone to London. His explanation to Marian is confused. He uses the word 'tackled', saying that it means 'bringing a man down' (p. 226). Marian's reaction is vividly given – 'Her face had gone white and her eyes were like dark holes in a sheet of ice' (p. 226). Marian implies that Hugh is staunch and that Ted is easily influenced. Having used the word 'blackmail' herself, Marian tells Leo that she will tell Hugh she won't marry him if Ted goes to the war. Leo feels secure at last when he tells Marian that Hugh does not know about the messages and is merely being patriotic in trying to get Ted to join up. The tension is rising, and there is pathos too when Leo asks Marian why she can't marry Ted. All the class awareness, and possibly the commercial arrangement (the Maudsleys go on renting Brandham Hall if Marian marries Hugh) is in her answer. When she breaks down, her tears move Leo to see her as *his* Marian, not the deceiver, but 'Marian of the Zodiac, Marian whom I loved' (p. 228). Afterwards Leo becomes deceiver by altering the time of the message. Both he and Marian have forgotten the tea party next day in celebration of Leo's birthday.

CHAPTER 21, *pp. 230–41*

The reconciliation with Marian has the effect of raising Leo's morale, but he has now learned sufficient about life to know that there is no certainty that things will continue to go well. He is still worried about what will happen: 'I feared for Lord Trimingham, I wept with Marian, but for Ted I grieved' (p. 231). His relationship with Ted is 'the tribute of one nature to another' (p. 231), but he finds Ted to blame for what has happened, since nothing can ever be a lady's fault. He thinks of Ted's power over Marian as 'He had cast a spell on her' (p. 232). Leo feels that Marian will not wait for Ted in the outhouse because he knows that one of her characteristics is impatience. His imaginary dialogue in anger between them shows how imaginative he is. Leo describes the Ted–Marian relationship as 'a parasite of the emotions' (p. 233), thus linking it with the deadly nightshade. Leo determines on the spell to break Ted's influence, but is careful to insist that it will not do harm to the individuals. He foresees Marian and Ted recognizing their positions and not stepping across the class and social barriers. For Leo to work the spell successfully he must be fearful himself. He therefore chooses to take on the deadly nightshade. He is desperately afraid of what he has to do, and nearly succumbs to the temptation to return and ask Mrs Maudsley if he may listen to the music.

Again there is a high level of narrative tension, because Leo outside makes a noise which Denys is sent to investigate. There is also the fear that he – Leo – may be shut out for the night. Notice Leo's careful preparation of the spell, and notice also that he is assembling *facts* rather than trying to deal with human emotions. He is very serious. We should also notice the emphasis on the word 'thirteen', which refers to the spell, to Mrs Maudsley's private superstition, and to Leo's age. The first sight of the deadly nightshade has strong sexual suggestions, though not evident to Leo – 'It was like a lady standing in her doorway looking out for someone' (p. 240). In a brilliant paragraph Hartley has the deadly nightshade nearly overcome Leo, who almost welcomes the assault but panics, the whole experience – like the experience of sex he is to see the next evening – being too much for him. He just remembers the Latin words of the spell, but although he destroys the plant, in a sense it has destroyed him. He ends up on his back, with grains of earth dropping on his face. This is also descriptive of death.

CHAPTER 22, *pp. 242–51*

Even such a casual remark as people going mad connects with Mrs Maudsley. The change in the weather marks the end of Leo's fantasy – he feels that he has purged himself of this. He also feels in his new age that he is another person, and he is ashamed of his magician's reputation and of writing to his mother. He feels almost adult, but this is another delusion, and he ponders on the way he has been treated both as a little boy and as a little man, with Marian having 'endowed me with the importance of a grown-up' (p. 245). He finds himself admiring Marcus for his interest in people – though Marcus's interest is not 'to imagine about them' (p. 246) which, of course, is one of Leo's main interests. Leo's decision to wear his Norfolk suit instead of his green suit is an attempt to establish his identity. The letter from Mrs Colston shows her concern for Leo, her doubts about whether what she did was right, and her fear of offending the Maudsleys. There is a strong sense of what-might-have-been about this. The bad taste of the second present (a tie) is redeemed by Trimingham's generous gesture in taking it and putting it on, thus counteracting Marcus's 'deepening frown' (p. 249). Leo is moved and keeps the tie for years. There is grim humour in the exchange between Denys and his mother, while Marcus's comments on the tie make Leo aware of his real status, or lack of it. He hasn't the nerve to go back to the scene of his crime, to see if the 'corpse of the plant' (p. 250) has been put on the rubbish heap or somehow found its way there. His new identity is flat and, aware of this, he changes back into his green suit. He is thus ready for the tragic climax of his role as go-between.

CHAPTER 23, *pp. 252–62*

In the last chapter of the novel to be set in Leo's past, events move quickly. Leo is dismayed by Marian's putting a letter in his hand, but before he can do anything about it he finds himself playing a scuffling game with her which he enjoys. Mrs Maudsley's interruption of this is dramatic and penetrating – she sees into and through Marian's lies, and obviously determines to attack the weaker of the two, Leo. He soon reveals that he can't remember where Nannie Robson lives. Mrs Maudsley shows her cunning, for by taking him into the garden she is encouraging him to talk, which he does. He realizes he may be on the edge of giving something away when he speaks of the deadly nightshade (after all he knows that Marian and Ted meet nearby). Before he knows where he is Mrs Maudsley has proved more potent than the plant. Her threat to get the gardener to take the note is the first of a series of questions or implications which demonstrate that Leo is lying. In a superb dramatic climax, the thunder comes, and the memory of the older Leo fails him in trying to establish exactly what was said. Leo's flight to his room, now occupied by the possessions of another guest, shows him without peace. For Leo there is no escape. At the tea table we notice that Mrs Maudsley has the same ability to deceive as Marian, for she is all friendliness to Leo, obviously because she is going to use him to discover Marian's intrigue with Ted. Mrs Maudsley's tension is shown by the shaking of hands, the general tension over Marian's non-arrival by the pauses after what is said, and Leo's tension by his inability to swallow his piece of cake. The pulling of the crackers takes on an almost hysterical force, the butler's report that Marian has not been at Nannie Robson's adds to this, and Leo himself ('my insides began to revolt anew') feels that the faces around him have 'a wild, hobgoblin look' (p. 260). Mrs Maudsley's decision to act cuts with full dramatic force across the party atmosphere, Mr Maudsley's calling her name being a last attempt to make her behave in a balanced way. Her seizing of Leo is demon-like. She is possessed, and she knows where she is going. The heat has broken, the rain has come, and all is revealed. Leo's seeing Ted and Marian as the Water-Carrier and the Virgin shows him still in the grip of his spell. He says that he is 'more mystified than horrified' (p. 262) and this fits exactly with his consistent inability to understand 'spooning'. With an imaginative child's sensitivity he is scared by the shadow on the wall and by the hysteria of Mrs Maudsley. Her screams destroy any normal sexual feelings for him in the future. Ted's shooting himself is the tragic postscript to the action.

EPILOGUE, *pp. 263–81*

The Epilogue has been criticized as unnecessary. There is no doubt however that the reader wants to know what the effect of the close look into diary and memory has been. There are hints throughout the action, but the rest of the story has still to be told. It is told here – the mental breakdown, the return to school, the blockage caused by guilt which has frustrated normal development in the boy and the adult. Notice how, in his mental illness, Leo shuts off from the reality he has known, so that 'the tidings of Ted's suicide came to me voicelessly, like a communication in a dream' (p. 263). Leo is greatly moved by that death, but with regard to the Brandham Hall people he feels 'vanquished, and for ever' (p. 264). He states that the spell worked – it broke the relationship of Ted and Marian–but he recognizes that it has rebounded on him. He has been punished by the supernatural powers and by fate, because he has tried to set 'the Zodiac against itself' (p. 264). Leo comes to reject people or, as he epigrammatically puts it, 'the life of facts proved no bad substitute for the facts of life' (p. 265). This is pathetic, but the explanation is logical to Leo. He thought that Ted had paid with his life for spooning. Leo can never get over that fact or ever want to spoon. The finest dramatic stroke of the Epilogue is Leo's discovery of Marian's last letter to Ted, still sealed. Expectation of what will be revealed is held in the balance by the adult Leo. He now realizes that Marian did like him before he became her go-between, and that perhaps Ted 'was the only one who had had a true impulse of contrition' (p. 266). He works out what has happened, and decides that his guilt feelings immediately after the events and his thinking himself without blame in his adulthood were equally wrong. He rejects the spell – he cannot take it seriously, since it was not a fact – but he thinks about the 'others' and fears to know what has happened. He compares the inmates of Brandham Hall to 'figures in a picture' (p. 268) and wants to leave them that way. But the opening of Marian's final letter gives them a terrible and moving reality, and he feels compelled to return to Brandham. He overcomes superstition, and he acquires the facts: of Hugh's death and of Ted's (nominally Hugh's) son's death, the latter having been given the second name of 'Maudsley'. Intent on his memories, and having prayed in church, the older Leo now meets, unexpectedly and dramatically, Ted's grandson, the present Lord

Trimingham. For a moment the latter fears discovery but Leo, who can still lie, pretends that the real Lord Trimingham was this young man's grandfather. The old Marian has become forgetful, just as Nannie Robson was supposed to have been, and she lives in Nannie Robson's old home. Real, too, is the fact that the village hall, the scene of Leo's triumph, does not stand out in any way in his mind when he sees it. There is pathos in Marian's lonely life, and little doubt that because of her misdemeanour she and Hugh were not much visited by society. The play on the word 'Hugh' continues even here, but at least Leo learns all the facts about what actually happened in the few days after the scene in the outhouse. Mrs Maudsley suffered from religious madness, and Mr Maudsley restored order. Marian admits that her grandson thinks that he is under a 'spell' (p. 278). She also (wrongly) thinks that Leo must have appreciated the beauty of her love-affair with Ted. Leo lies, and says he did appreciate it, and then hears Marian attack 'this hideous century' (p. 279) which he as a little boy had believed was the Golden Age. The final action sees Leo being employed in his boy's role of go-between. Before that Marian, only recognizable because of the 'frosty fire' in her eyes (p. 275), has insight enough to see that Leo is 'all dried up inside' (p. 280). Her words to Leo are insensitive when she observes, 'there's no spell or curse except an unloving heart' (p. 280). We are reminded of the opening sentence of the novel, when Leo calls himself 'a foreigner in the world of the emotions' (p. 280). And just as he was compelled in those far-off days to take messages despite what he came to learn, so, though he marvels at Marian's 'self-deception' (p. 280) the fascination, the spell, still exists; and the 'south-west prospect of the Hall' (p. 281) doubtless brings back to Leo that intense heat, the romance, the fantasy and the terrible reality of his role as go-between.

Characters

LEO COLSTON

Leo is a complex character. His reactions are seen in two ways. Leo in his mid-sixties finds the diary of events at Brandham Hall for a period in the summer vacation of 1900. This leads him to a search – through the associations of memory which the diary reveals – for an explanation of his subsequent life, a life devoted to facts instead of people. The boy Leo is therefore seen throughout with the hindsight of the older Leo. Sometimes the representation of him is graphic, immediate, as if the events in which the boy is involved are occurring in a present time. They aren't, and from time to time there is a remark from the adult narrator which comments on or bridges the gap between the past and the present.

Leo is something of an outsider both at school and at Brandham Hall. The only child of a widowed mother and a bank-manager father, he shows the influence of both of them. Hartley is intent on emphasizing this. Leo's father was a book-collector: Leo spends his adult life cataloguing books, working in libraries, his work the facts by which he has chosen to live. I say 'chosen' because the childhood experience which shapes his later life provides him with the choice of encountering people on an *emotional* level (which he fears) or withdrawing from personal relationships (which he does). The boy Leo is also like his mother. Just as she, before her widowhood, delights in social display so Leo, arrived at Brandham Hall, finds himself in a world inhabited, in his mind, by superior beings, gods and goddesses, creatures he connects with the zodiac of his spells. Leo is naturally anxious to please, anxious not to offend and anxious to observe the rules of good behaviour.

When Leo goes to Brandham Hall (though at the last minute he panics and asks his mother to write and say that he is ill) he is armed with the success of his spells. Perhaps we shouldn't forget that he has been 'vanquished' by his more normal school fellows in the past. Leo is an exceptional boy – highly intelligent (note his feeling for words), superstitious, imaginative, impressionable, easily hurt and sexually ignorant. The impression given is that his father was too withdrawn to tell him the facts of life. His mother – remember the period, in which open mention of sex would not be considered respectable – would not have said anything to him anyway. The result is that Leo is advanced intellectually and imaginatively but does not understand colloquial and slang meanings. His inquiring mind wants to *know*, and at particular crises at Brandham Hall he tries to discover the 'facts' which he so delights in storing. Unlike the more sophisticated Marcus, he manages to get the wrong idea about 'spooning', associating it with the picture distortions of the popular seaside postcards. Whereas the normal boy would pick up smutty sexual ideas and retail them with enjoyment, Leo knows and understands little about sex. His romantic and idealized love for Marian is based on service: where using his bathing suit to dry Marian's hair is happiness, where singing with her as accompanist is an expression of love, where having her ask him if he wants money is anguish, and where reading her few words of love for Ted is desolation. All these show Leo's sensitive, unprotected, defenceless, innocent and immature nature. For him experience is suffering, half-awareness, or incomprehensible phrases.

Consider Leo's reactions to Brandham Hall. The early days find him contemplating his surroundings, hardly able to put names to people, learning how to behave, conscious of what not to do because of Marcus's standards. He must not come down to breakfast in slippers, not pick up the clothes he drops in the bedroom. The constant coming and going of anonymous house guests, the lawns and croquet, the formality of morning prayers, the lavish amounts of food: all these give Leo that sense of social advancement which puts him in the frame of mind to become a go-between. This role is also a sign of elevation, for doesn't Lord Trimingham name him Mercury, the messenger of the gods? Leo is very impressionable. Just as he was an outsider at school before the spells (and after that he was to be feared), so he is the outsider at Brandham who becomes an important secret insider. Marian is an opportunist who sees Leo's usefulness; he paves the way so that her own love-affair with Ted will have a somewhat easier passage. Leo is ignorant of this, but the heat now becomes his friend with Marian's purchase of his lightweight suit. This present is most important to our understanding of Leo. Not only does it confirm Marian's interest in him (and ensure that he will do anything for her), it also confers upon Leo a new status, a sense of moving in the same pure and socially acceptable world as his 'gods and goddesses' at Brandham Hall.

I have said that Leo is sensitive and impressionable, and in relation to both Ted and Marian this is obvious. Both, in their different ways, are tender to him, though Ted's concern is certainly the warmer. Both bandage his knee, but Ted tries to dress the later wound of frustrated ignorance and injured love. Leo also likes being different, likes being solitary, delights in exploring situations, in teasing out meanings, in asking himself interminable questions; often, because of his innocence (or ignorance), he finds no satisfactory answers. We are asked to believe that a thirteen-year-old public-school boy with a feeling for words, highly intelligent, superstitious but methodical, with some scientific inclinations, would be ignorant of a wide range of colloquialisms, would not know who Shylock was, and would connect 'spooning' with seaside postcards. I think we can accept this because of the period and the degree of sexual reserve involved. Also, Hartley has given us in Leo a boy with recognizable problems *before* he sees the love-making scene between Ted and Marian. These problems have been indicated above, and I would suggest that the reason Leo runs from emotions in adult life is because he is *frightened* of his own emotions, which he associates with past death (Ted's) and past breakdowns (his own). The adult Leo observes that it was not what he saw that upset him, but Mrs Maudsley's screams. Her hysteria sets him on the path to breakdown.

Leo in the past was 'vanquished', reduced to solitary tears and frustration, near breakdown, saved by the spell which 'produced' such lucky (for him) results. Then, upset at the thought of going to Brandham, he pleads the excuse of illness. We should note the idea of illness in the presentation of Leo; he is always aware of its possibilities, whether mental or physical refuge is being sought. He cries when Marian cries; he is terribly upset when he knows that Ted is upset. He goes as near as he can to emotional experience with the deadly nightshade. The terrible thing is that the mutilation of the plant is self-mutilation as well, for it is this experience from which Leo does not recover. He is now no match for the deadly nightshade of Mrs Maudsley or that offshoot of the same plant, Marian. Her pushing Leo the next day over the final letter is a kind of rough-and-tumble echo of Leo's struggle with the plant. Mrs Maudsley's seizing him and taking him into the garden, later propelling him through the rain to the outhouse because he knows where Marian is, also reflects the previous night's battle. When the heat breaks, Leo is broken. By acting as go-between, and being puffed up by the experience, Leo is trapped in the spell he has woven around the immortals of Brandham Hall. They are mortal, snobbish, cunning, neurotic and self-interested. Leo is on the edge of sexual, moral and social education. He is a curious mixture of the adult in the boy, though with the older Leo as narrator, he is the boy in the adult as well. He is corrupted by adult standards, and adopts them himself. His spells are a retreat from life, an inability to face the defeats of common experience.

Because Court Place has none of the grandeur that is Brandham Hall, Leo has something of an inferiority complex – which Marian's attentions, his secret role of go-between and his achievements (the catch and the singing) quickly reduce. But he is interested in people as people – he has much natural warmth and *he needs to be accepted by them*. His reactions to Ted reflect the divisions within him. Ted is 'only' a farmer, but he is much more than that to the boy whose knee he bandages. He represents the strongly physical and the unexplained sexual which the boy fears, but Leo also recognizes that in some ways he wants to be like Ted when he grows up. When Leo asks Marian why she can't marry Ted, though he really knows that such a class barrier cannot be crossed, his question shows his own sympathetic belief that she should be free to do so. But he thinks of the Golden Age which the twentieth century will bring, and he sees the marriage of Trimingham and Marian as one between a god and a goddess. Moreover, despite his feeling for Ted (which is close to love), he also feels for Hugh. The latter treats him throughout with gentlemanly respect and consideration, is always the model of good breeding whether he is asking Leo to take a message, telling him to come on in the cricket match, inviting him into the smoking-room, or merely looking disappointed at one of Marian's rebuffs. Leo wants to serve him, wants to make all well, and there is no more telling indication of the nature of his character than in the fantasy where, after his spell has worked, he sees in imagination Ted noticing Marian merely as a pretty girl who is beyond his reach and Marian, learning that Ted is a farmer, not wishing to know him because of the difference in their status. We all have our fantasies and our hopes, and the fact is that Leo indulges his because the prospect of reality – death and division in his mind (he even believes that Ted may murder Trimingham) – is too terrible to contemplate and *impossible* to live through.

There is little doubt that Marian rules Ted, that Mrs Maudsley rules her children (Marian being a rebel) and that Leo himself is somewhat easily ruled. He is impressed by most people he meets, and even the gnome-like Mr Maudsley comes to register with Leo as a man whose appearance is deceptive and whose strength in moments of crisis – his innings in the cricket match, his control during his wife's breakdown – is crucial. Leo's desire to please, that he wishes to be thought well of, means that he will do what he knows he shouldn't do. Sometimes this is pathetic, as when he falsifies the time Ted gives him for the final meeting with Marian. This is the little boy who thinks that because Marian is impatient she will reject Ted if she is kept waiting for five minutes! When he opens her letter to Ted, fifty-two years after she wrote it, he realizes his error when he reads 'I shall be there at six, and wait till seven or eight or nine or Doomsday' (p. 268). It was indeed Doomsday – for Leo, for Marian, for Ted and for Mrs Maudsley, who goes mad.

At other times Leo blunders, but we must never forget that he is a boy who wants adults to like him, who tries to sort out their problems in the only way which has proved effective in the past – through the spell which puts everything right. The boy who slides down the straw-stack, who serves Ted by oiling his bat, who makes the game-winning catch and who sings with moving purity the songs at the concert, has an over-active mind, but so many gaps in his basic knowledge of life that he is wounded, frustrated by his ignorance. He has too an obstinacy and pride which tell against him at important moments – his running away from the farm when Ted grows angry and his rejection of Ted's offer to tell him about spooning. At other times he is quick-witted, as when he heads off Marcus from the outhouses (when they have heard the lovers talking) by saying that this is boring. There is something refreshing and natural in his humorous exchanges with Marcus in their private language and pseudo-French. At the time he is unaware of Marcus's motive, though the adult Leo now knows him to be his mother's spy. This shows Leo as a boy enjoying the give and take of verbal battle, free from the emotional scars inflicted on him when he meddles in the adult world. He shows that he has both wit and humour of an attractive nature. Nor should we forget Leo's account of the adults when he is not indulging his private dreams of their divine qualities. His reports of Denys being put in his place by Mrs Maudsley have a certain quiet malice.

No account of Leo can encompass everything, for in a sense his character spans the whole length of the novel. The interested reader will find more than is suggested in this sketch here. Everything Leo thinks and does reveals something of his nature. We see him as a boy in an adult world, and the narrative is about what he thinks, how he responds, what he knows and, sadly, what he doesn't know. Leo is a clever psychological study in innocence and mental ability. His presentation is consistent throughout. The roots of his behaviour and reactions are to be found in that tellingly brief but most important account of his parents. The adult Leo buries the past, but once he opens the grave there is, to use his word, a resurrection. The Leo he was faces the Leo he is, and the sixty-five-year-old Leo goes back to Brandham, his interest in people as distinct from facts at last reborn by the diary and memory. In taking the final message to Ted's grandson Leo is repairing not only Marian's futile life but his own. *People* are reality, facts are the substitute for living. In the end, perhaps, Leo has learned more than he has lost. He may be dried up, but he has come to terms with himself.

MARIAN

All the characters in *The Go-Between* are seen through the eyes of Leo the boy and through the hindsight of Leo the man. Marian can be seen as a selfish girl who exploits Leo cruelly in her own interests; she can also be seen as an opportunist who likes Leo but uses him to further her love-affair with Ted Burgess. Marian is like her mother (and her father, but more of this later). She is also a victim of the class/society/

social divisions of her time. It is essential from her family's point of view as tenants of Brandham Hall that she marry Lord Trimingham. By doing so she raises the status of herself and her family. Marian will get a badly scarred and, by her standards, a rather boring lover instead of the sexually attractive though socially unacceptable Ted Burgess. Marian survives bitterly into old age. She may be compared with Leo, who has also survived though with inward scars which cannot be erased. Marian's role in the novel is both pathetic and selfish. There is little doubt that she finds the society at Brandham Hall boring, and that her affair with Ted is stimulating, the more so for being secret.

She is described by Marcus as being beautiful. We notice that there is a clash of wills between herself and her mother. Leo refers to Marian as hooded and hawk-like. She and her mother are formidable, but the likeness does not end there. Marian gives evidence of being neurotic, irritable, worried, her mind elsewhere. She is also cunning, as is her mother, for she takes precautions not to be discovered. There is the occasion when she plays with Leo over the last letter, and there are the lies about her visiting Nannie Robson and about Nannie Robson's memory fading. But she is also like her father. In simple language, he is the survivor who is always prepared to take responsibility. It is notable that the old Marian reveals a like toughness after the discovery of her affair with Ted. She survives, but her mother is put away. She has held her head high through the obvious gossip.

Marian is connected with the deadly nightshade. As the plant grows out of the outhouse and spreads, so Marian's intrigue spreads and enters the soul of Leo. At first, none of this is apparent to Leo. The trip to Norwich to buy him a suit is apparently a sympathetic and generous gesture, though later Leo realizes that she had made the shopping expedition the excuse for a secret meeting with Ted Burgess. She has beaten her mother here, for she had refused Mrs Maudsley's request to wait until Trimingham had arrived. This is evidence of her strong will. When she receives Ted's first note, Marian, dressing Leo's injured knee, is greatly moved, so much so that she forgets she has just bandaged Leo's knee when she returns from having quickly read the note. Yet she is worried too. Her emphasis on secrecy reveals her fear. She threatens anger, retracts it, is obviously jittery. Perhaps she can sense her mother's suspicions.

Whether that is true or not, Marian now proceeds to plan after this first opportunity has presented itself. She tells Mrs Maudsley that Leo would be much happier on his own rather than in grown-up company, and the dozing Leo overhears her suggesting that the ball could be put off if Marcus has measles. This implies that Marian has no wish to become engaged if it can be delayed, and that the times remaining to her with Ted are precious. The 'Hugh', 'who' and 'you' confusion finds Marian snappy, but when she realizes that she has hurt Leo she speaks kindly to him, whether from self-interest or because she likes him is not clear. She certainly guides the conversation in order to persuade him to take the reply to Ted, and deceives Leo by telling him that it is 'on business matters' (p. 99). She at first refuses to watch the croquet and then agrees to go when she sees that Leo is disappointed. Once again she is showing her inclination; staying away means rejection of Hugh, going means acceptance of her lot in life. But Marian is clever enough, as she shows often, to appear to be enjoying Hugh's company when her mind is elsewhere.

Marian suggests that Leo stays much longer, and considers it settled. It is almost as if she is pressing on in a kind of wild impetuosity which is bound to lead to discovery. She brushes off Hugh with the hurtful reply that she will sing at the concert if he will, and her emotion during the cricket match is evident to Leo. At the peak of Ted's innings she is too moved to speak – 'Her eyes were bright, her cheeks were flushed, and her lips trembled' (p. 135). When Ted walks into the pavilion alone, in triumph, Marian is so overcome that she does not raise her eyes – to do so would be to reveal her feelings before her ever-observant mother.

There is something rebellious in Marian, for her playing at the concert is an act of open defiance. Marian's move through the audience to the piano is decisive, so much so that it disconcerts Ted himself, who, of course, cannot give himself away since they are both on social view. In a sense this is Marian's way of crossing the class barrier. But later Leo hears her singing 'Home, Sweet Home'. She has given in again, aware of the need to be seen to be doing what will please Hugh (we remember that it is his request).

With this constant tension in her life as she moves nearer to her formal engagement, there is every reason to account for her reaction when Leo says that he can't take her next letter to Ted. She is very angry ('her body curved to pounce' p. 166), and calls Leo a 'little Shylock' (p. 167), unaware in her temper that she is injuring a child.

This anticipates, and here is the family likeness again, her mother's pouncing on Leo in the final terrible sequence. By tea Marian has recovered, for her second thoughts have told her to put on the act and be friendly to Leo (and Trimingham), though Leo doesn't wait to see what her unspoken message is. When she does see Leo on her return from London she apologizes for slanging him, saying 'really I'm a good-natured girl' (p. 223). She reacts with temper and authority when she learns that Ted may go into the army at Trimingham's suggestion. Marian never lacks spirit, but after she has said that she won't marry Trimingham if Ted does go, there is the terrible feeling of compulsion, and she breaks down when she says 'I've *got* to!' (p. 228). There is no surer way of winning back her postman.

The vitality and the attempts to express independence are part of her character, but there is no reason to doubt her love for Ted which, while it springs from sexual passion, does not diminish with passing time but is seen in her feelings for her grandson. Over those years, with only the past to look back on, she has built a wall of self-deception around herself. She is lonely, but talks of visitors. She idealizes her love for Ted, is very conscious of being the Lady Trimingham, but retains a kind of honesty. She acts thoughtlessly, perhaps even a shade cruelly to Leo, when she tells him that he must tell her grandson 'there's no spell or curse except an unloving heart' (p. 280). It is pathetic to find her living in the past because of the coldness of the present, and Leo is treated with the same lack of real consideration for his feelings as he was as a boy. Marian tells him 'we trusted you with our great treasure' (p. 279). No doubt the selfishness of this shines through her frosty eyes to the older Leo. Thoroughly selfish and acting from self-will, Marian young had some sympathetic warmth, but Marian old has none.

TED BURGESS

In some ways Ted Burgess is the character triumph of *The Go-Between* — wild, a lady-killer, a natural cricketer, as opportunist as Marian *but*, and it is a very important but, warm and sensitive to the boy he knows has been injured by the secret affair between himself and Marian. When he catches Leo after the slide down the straw-stack he is initially angry, but this is soon over when he realizes that the boy is from the hall, and also that he is hurt. Leo offers to do anything for him after his knee has been dressed. Ted, with some caution, takes this opportunity to begin the series of messages between himself and Marian.

Ted is seen throughout the novel in contrast to Trimingham and, but for being caught out by 'our postman', he would have triumphed over him completely on the cricket field. But Ted is not in control of his own fate. He is a tenant farmer, very popular in the neighbourhood, but he cannot cross the class barriers any more than Marian can. He suffers under the pressures of his affair with Marian. He knows that she is going to marry Trimingham, and Leo notices some deterioration in Ted and the fact that he has lost weight, presumably because of the worry. There is the pressure of being asked by Trimingham to join the army to fight the Boers, and thus give up not only Marian but his means of livelihood. However Ted is still balanced: he does 'get his rag out', yet he shows Leo consideration – not just, I think, because he can be used, but because he sees the boy's innocence and bewilderment. He also sees that Leo can be hurt by Marian, and because of this Ted sympathizes with him. He appreciates Leo's bravery over his injured knee, and he tries to explain the relationship he has with Marian as 'business' and, honestly, 'It's more than that' (p. 85) when Leo asks him if it is a secret. But Ted is down-to-earth; he spoils Leo's romantic idea of his mission by telling him that if he can't give Marian the letter he's to 'put it in the place where you pull the chain' (p. 86).

Ted has a good sense of humour, a natural wit which contrasts with the mannered and dry utterances of Trimingham and Mr Maudsley. He offers to have the straw-stack 'combed and brushed for you' (p. 87) and excites Leo's curiosity about him, though all he can learn from the coachman is that Ted's 'a bit of a lad' (p. 93). When Ted finds out that Leo doesn't intend to bring any more letters he cleverly plays on Leo's softness and his feelings for Marian in order to maintain his own contact with her. He is concerned for his animals, but in seeking to keep Leo acting as go-between he refers to 'spooning' and then has to deal with Leo's sharpness and ignorance at the same time. Ted reveals his own moral standards with a frank honesty, though he is put out at the thought that spooning may lead to a baby. He is careful of Leo's sensitivity, but he achieves what he wants, for Leo agrees to act as the postman again.

The cricket match is Ted's high point of achievement. We note his boyish enthusiasm, and the fact that his unorthodox batting is successful right up until the last moment, a success which may be compared to his love-making with Marian. His innings shows a sheer physical strength, and a zest for enjoyment which is like his sexual drive for Marian. He is dismissed within sight of victory, and this perhaps hints at the flaw in the man, seen later when he shoots himself rather than fight on. The old Marian cynically observes, 'He should have waited till it all blew over' (p. 276). The concert reflects Ted's popularity, but he is uncomfortable in his suit and his public performance with Marian, so that he fights shy of an encore. He does sing again however, though his responses are clumsy enough to cause comment at this ladies' man being so shy with a lady. With Leo he is generous in his praise of the catch and modest about his own performance. The concert makes Ted all the more aware of the social divisions between himself and Marian, and his rough manner is a cover for his sensitive feelings. Unlike Marian, he cannot act.

Ted shows Leo genuine kindness. Further upset after Marian's attack on him, Leo once more presents himself to Ted. Noticing the evidence of tears, Ted sensitively tries to distract the boy from his grief, referring to the brilliant catch, taking him outside to watch him (Ted) pepper the rooks, interesting him in the gun, encouraging him to oil the bat. Ted will not tell Leo about spooning because 'it might spoil it for you' (p. 176) he says in all sincerity, not realizing that he and Marian are the very means of spoiling it for Leo for life. Then he 'gets his rag out', but he has the character to apologize, although Leo suspects that here Ted was motivated to get him to deliver more messages. Ted is weaker than Marian. He intends to do what she wants. Perhaps we remember him best of all in his natural exchanges with Leo, and certainly at the farm, in the kitchen, in the fields. He is caught up in something he cannot control. His final wave to Leo seems to convey his warmth. His suicide is a comment on a class system which makes any lasting relationship between himself and Marian impossible.

LORD TRIMINGHAM

Lord Trimingham is a gentleman and contrasts at every point with Ted Burgess. Wounded in the Boer War, scarred for life, he represents, with his mannered and leisurely way of life, the status – that of the hereditary aristocracy – which Mrs Maudsley wants for Marian. Hugh has a studied, well-bred presence. Since he can't afford to live at Brandham Hall he lets it to the Maudsleys, perhaps with an understanding that he and Marian shall become engaged.

Trimingham has severe limitations, although he is kind to Leo. He lacks liveliness, and one of the significant scenes in the novel finds him in the smoking-room with its suggestive pictures, the retreat for the males of the period. The cricket match symbolizes Trimingham's trial of strength with Ted. For all Denys's comments on the elegance and style of Trimingham's batting, he makes only a modest score, though it is off Hugh's bowling that Ted is caught by Leo. Trimingham spends his time attending the accepted society gatherings, only Marian's fascination keeping him from Goodwood. Yet there is something pathetic about his love, for he is dependent on Marian's response, and Marian is swift to change her mood – from being sweet and doing what her parents want her to do, to rejecting their wishes and flying in the face of convention. Trimingham is hurt by her refusal to sing unless he does, though Leo does his best to persuade him that this is a joke. Trimingham can't sing, and we feel that he represents impotence and elegance without life.

Trimingham is considerate to Leo. There is no cunning in his employing of Leo as a messenger to Marian. Nevertheless he does so, but he treats Leo throughout with a kind of even courtesy, as a grown-up, and with respect for the boy's feelings. It is Trimingham's style and status which raise Leo in his own mind, and after his initial jealousy over Trimingham's coming engagement to Marian, Leo is glad of it. After all, Leo is Mercury to the gods, and Trimingham has given him this official title. The viscount is completely lacking in arrogance and condescension to his tenants at Brandham, and although Mrs Maudsley makes a point of consulting him about her plans, he responds with a kind of courteous lack of interest. He is in the time-worn position of privilege which commands deference without effort, but he abuses it only once, as far as we can see, and that is when he approaches Ted in an attempt to persuade the latter to volunteer to fight against the Boers.

The old Marian reveals quite a lot about Trimingham. He loved her very much and the marriage shows him loyal to Marian, though he must have known, with the birth occurring seven months after the marriage, that the child was not his. Marian pays tribute to his staunchness, loyalty and silence. As he once said to Leo, 'Nothing is ever a lady's fault' (p. 161). Obviously he lives by this principle in his own life. He holds to a certain code of conduct, and if it is not flushed with emotion, at least it adds to his honour. Trimingham is likeable, with his wry sense of humour, but he represents the old century, its set way of life and its rigid class divisions. When he finds Marian and Leo together on one occasion – she is furtively passing Leo the unsealed letter – he affects to be interrupting a love-scene and asks if he may snatch Marian from Leo (Harold Pinter cleverly substituted the word 'gather' in the screenplay as being more fitting for a man like Trimingham to use). In other words, he behaves as if it is the most natural thing in the world. One wonders if this unruffled ease, carried into one's private emotional life, might not be more than a little monotonous to a partner of spirit.

MRS MAUDSLEY

I have already drawn attention to the family consistency with which Hartley presents his characters, and how Marian and her mother complement each other admirably in force of personality, excitability and determination to have their own way. Mrs Maudsley dominates, or appears to dominate. She favours Marcus, and almost certainly employs him as a spy (she lets him get up and move about again rather early after his illness) to see what he can find out about Marian through Leo. She has the measure of Denys, so that his pompous and waffling statements are cut down to size as she gets on with her job of running the household and organizing the day's activities. She is suspicious of Marian's activities, though she needs to question Leo in order to confirm them. Leo feels the power of her eyes, frightened of the 'beam from her eye, that black searchlight' (p. 49). Mrs Maudsley's casual remarks are loaded with suggestion. She urges Marian to delay her visit to Norwich until Trimingham arrives, thus ensuring that Marian will pay him the attention that his position and Marian's prospects demand. When Marian returns from Norwich and Leo shows off his suit, Mrs Maudsley pointedly asks if they met anyone in Norwich and Marian is dependent on Leo's hesitantly supportive reply. On the surface Mrs Maudsley treats Leo with kindness and pays him considerate attention, but there is an ominous quality about her presence which he undoubtedly feels. Her snobbery, her attempts to compel Marian, her relentless seizure of Leo after she has seen him put Marian's final letter in his pocket, are indications of her power.

What is not so clear is her illness, though Marcus goes some way to explaining that she is neurotic. The final incident in the outhouse drives her mad. She contrasts with her husband, who displays very little emotion, though he obviously deplores her action in seizing Leo and leaving the birthday tea by exclaiming the single word 'Madeleine!' (p. 261). She is obviously insecure despite her social command and graces, and it is apparent that she has set her heart on Marian having Trimingham (she always defers to Hugh but never to anybody else) since this will secure her a higher and permanently secure social status.

MR MAUDSLEY

This is a masterly character-study, achieved more by what is not said than what is. Leo calls him 'gnome-like' and is rather sarcastic about his trail of gold, since Mr Maudsley is a successful city man. He appears regularly to check the thermometer, is usually noncommittal and makes conventional remarks when he does so; and apart from family prayers, he leaves the household affairs to his capable wife. But he is deceptive (not deceiving), for crisis produces the best in him, and he reveals hidden depths at the concert when he makes a witty speech which brings in a reference to nearly every player – no mean achievement. For instance, he calls Leo the David who slew Goliath of Black Farm with a catch (Mr Maudsley unconsciously projects the end of the novel for, being 'caught out' by Mrs Maudsley through Leo, Ted goes home and slays himself). Mr Maudsley's innings is a triumph; he accumulates runs (perhaps he has accumulated money in the same discreet if rather plodding way) and, offended by Denys's wrong-headed attempts to save him from tiring himself, runs Denys out. His innings ensures that the hall stands a good chance of winning, his speech at the concert carries a wide currency of appreciation, and his smoking-room conversation with Trimingham in Leo's presence adds to Leo's confusion about Ted having a woman. But beneath his few words there is an astute mind, and one suspects that he sees into people with telling accuracy. After his wife is taken away his character restores things at Brandham Hall, for he has Marian's capacity to survive and an obstinacy of character which makes him ignore criticism.

MARCUS

If Leo is mentally precocious, Marcus, a year younger than Leo, is more experienced in the colloquial ways of the world which he can interpret where Leo can't. Marcus is a snob, in fact he and Denys are presented in some ways as caricatures of public-school types of the period. Marcus is conventional to the point of absurdity, enjoying telling Leo not to pick up his clothes and not to wear slippers to breakfast. He even tells Leo what he should wear and should not wear for the cricket match, for Marcus is knowledgeable about dress and behaviour. He has a sensitive nose: that is, all those who don't live at the hall or visit at the hall, smell. He is sometimes in error, as when he thinks that Leo living at Court Place means perhaps a superior residence. Marcus's illness is important to the plot. Leo is thrown into the company of Marian and Trimingham and, through his freedom in going to the farm, Ted. His mother's favourite, Marcus recovered is his mother's spy. He is a gossip, and one suspects that he is not put off by Leo's manoeuvre near the outhouses, for he knows there is a couple spooning there. He can always be relied upon to tell which of the servants is in trouble. But it would be one-sided just to see Marcus as unpleasant. He is jealous of Leo's magic and his achievements in the cricket match and the concert, and he tries to put down Leo by talking in French. There is some genuine banter in the exchanges between the two boys, and some real humour too. Marcus tells Leo that his mother is neurotic, and that she has been made ill because she thinks that Marian may not honour her engagement to Trimingham. Marcus teases Leo, and is particularly insistent in his insulting emphasis on the word 'green'. He likes punning (witness 'awe-mongers') but is also cunning. He tricks Leo into revealing that he knows where Marian is. His tale-telling, we suspect, is why Mrs Maudsley seizes on Leo at the birthday tea: she knows that he knows.

DENYS

Denys is caricature. Like Marcus he is a snob, but a snob born to condescend and to do what he thinks is the right thing. He is decent to Ted Burgess when he sees him swimming, having previously said that it was 'cheek' for anyone else to be using the bathing place. He acts as an irritant upon his mother, likes to hear the sound of his own voice, and is firmly put in his place daily by his mother and by his father in the cricket match. He obviously feels that Trimingham is the man on whom he should model himself, that one should buy one's ties at Challow and Crawshay's, that he is expected to have opinions, though these in fact turn out to be either stale borrowings or attempts to be childishly officious or even pompous. He is put out when his mother scrutinizes him closely. This parody of a public-school boy who has to have his say whatever kind of fool he makes of himself is at times a little cruel; but in presenting him as someone who is made by his society, saying its sayings and adopting its standards, Hartley is again underlining the class-riddled society which had so much status, and indeed so much economic power, at the time. Both Denys and Marcus are killed in the First World War.

Commentary

THEMES

Sexual Awakening

Apart from his mother, there is no mention of women or girls in Leo's life before he goes to Brandham Hall. For the first day or so there he hardly recognizes people as individuals, but after Marcus had told him that Marian is beautiful Leo studies her and is struck when 'she opened her eyes – I remember the sudden burst of blue – and her face lit up' (p. 37). His associations are still with the zodiac, but the misery of the 'mild persecution' (p. 42) because of his unsuitable clothes brings Marian directly into his life. She rescues him by the Norwich proposal, her disregard for money and, perhaps most important of all, their shared knowledge (prophetic of the bigger secret to come) that Leo's clothes are mended and that he has no summer clothes at home.

Although Leo the narrator says 'My spiritual transformation took place in Norwich' (p. 48) this is only part of the truth. Once arrayed in green, Leo is Robin Hood to Maid Marian, and the world of his imagination is filled with her. His idea is that of service, and he tells Trimingham that he would do anything for her. On the eve of his thirteenth birthday he thinks of himself as a man, but he is far from being so, not just in physical terms but in emotional ones as well. He does not understand his feelings, but he shows them in a kind of day-dream way. The heat which before was Leo's enemy becomes his friend, and at one stage he identifies the heat with Marian herself. All his exchanges with Marian reflect the beginnings of sexual awakening. When he takes the first letter to her she bandages his knee, a contact which he understands in the direct sense but not in the emotional one. Earlier Leo, not allowed to bathe but very observant of Ted Burgess's body and its power, makes a gesture of tenderness which shows that although he does not understand his feelings, he is expressing them unconsciously by the delightful action, with sexual and sensual feeling, of drying Marian's hair on his unused bathing suit. Leo's idea ('It pierced me with joy' p. 58) is followed by Marian's invitation to him to spread her hair without hurting her. Leo's response is 'how could I have hurt her? I had hardly touched her hair, much as I wanted to ... My thoughts enveloped her, they entered into her ... I felt my cup was full' (pp. 58–9). Significantly, Leo knows that he wants to be something to her, but he doesn't know what.

Marian moves Leo by her personal interest in him. She forgets that she has asked about his family, but apologizes in such a way that 'it gave me a strange feeling of sweetness and power' (p. 65). When Marian threatens Leo with anger if he breaks her injunction to secrecy he is 'very hurt and on the point of tears' (p. 89). Perhaps the most telling indication of his sexual awakening is his response to Marian asking him if he wants to take messages because he likes Ted. Leo tells her that there is another reason: 'I had no idea that when I came to them the words would be so difficult to say; but at last I brought them out. "Because I like you" ' (p. 100). The joy he feels cannot continue. When he reads Marian's words to Ted, Leo is disillusioned, but in part this is because his sexual knowledge is so limited, conditioned by the postcards and the grotesque 'thin-fat motif' (p. 111) which he associates with 'spooning'. Although his reactions against the thought of Marian and Ted spooning are real, he is still moved, under pressure from Ted, at the thought of making Marian cry. His cross-questioning of Ted about spooning reflects the urgency of his feelings, and at one stage this is so insistent that it exasperates Ted.

The concert is Leo's innocent sexual fulfilment in a way, just as his later wrestling with the deadly nightshade is a kind of sexual overthrow. This imaginative child at the moment of his triumph that night feels 'that I was undergoing these harsh experiences not only for Marian, but with her ... Together we confronted the fate worse than death; together we soared to our apotheosis' (p. 148). After this, Leo endures Marian's accusations when he refuses to take the next note to Ted, but even here his reflexes show his feelings, for he tries to 'push her away from me or to bring her closer' (p. 166), the gesture showing his love – fear reaction to what she is saying. When he arrives at Ted's Leo is still upset, not only with Marian, but at having no real idea of what 'spooning' or 'lover-like' means. Such are the pressures, however, that he feels a sense of freedom when he knows that she has gone to London, though he is (unconsciously) sexually stimulated when Marcus tells him: 'At the tolling of six o'clock the doors will be thrown open and she'll come in riding it, and wearing tights, she says, if Mama will let her, which I doubt. She may have to wear bloomers' (p. 210). Now Leo, because of his sisterless upbringing, is generally prudish, as he had shown in his reactions to the smoking-room pictures, but here he says that 'I closed my eyes against the enchanting vision and for a moment my old feeling for Marian came back' (p. 210). It is a revealing comment, the closing of the eyes expressing a kind of fear, the fear that the 'old feeling' will cause him emotional suffering again.

It does. When Marian breaks down after saying that she has to marry Trimingham, she becomes once more 'Marian whom I loved' (p. 228). And the boy who doesn't understand his feelings is further elated (and tortured) when 'she rose and kissed me; she had never kissed me before' (p. 229). The theme of sexual awakening runs throughout *The Go-Between* and culminates with the scene in the outhouse: for Leo, though initially mystified by this embrace of the Virgin and the Water-Carrier, obviously knows afterwards what he has seen. But before this there is a mockery of sexual coming together which contributes another twist to the theme. I refer to Marian's scuffle with Leo when she hands him the final letter which Mrs Maudsley spots. Leo says 'I didn't want to stop, I wanted to go on to a conclusion. Daring each other with our eyes we lunged and dodged and feinted ...' (p. 253). This is Hartley's brilliant way of revealing Leo's sexual stirrings which the boy cannot translate and, to be fair, feelings of which Marian is probably unaware. Mrs Maudsley is to press Leo on to the conclusion with its associations of fear and death, associations which are so strong that the older Leo's first reaction to seeing Marian again is expressive of his suffering, as 'The inhibitions of fifty years rose up in me, and took control of my face and voice' (p. 273).

Corruption of Innocence

Leo's rejection of Ted's offer to tell him about spooning contributes to the catastrophe. Indelibly linked to his sexual awakening is a loss of innocence, for he has come to Brandham without any knowledge of sex except the postcard associations referred to above. Marcus instructs him to an extent, but he seems to have an inbred puritanical spirit, as when he reacts with distaste to the smoking-room picture of the woman's breasts pressed against the back of the gambler's chair. His innocence is abused and bruised by Marian and Ted, but not, I think, with intent. Marian herself seems unaware, apart from her spurt of rage, about what she is doing to Leo. Her self-deceptive nature credits Leo with understanding and appreciating the precious treasure of her love for Ted and his for her. It takes no account fifty-two years later of the terrible scars inflicted on a boy who is faced with a reality which leads to his having a breakdown and then a broken life.

This theme of the corruption of innocence is handled in a number of ways by Hartley. Ted and Marian use Leo, getting around him when he backs away from taking their messages, or raging at him as Marian does with unjust accusations which cause the boy tremendous inward suffering. Ted, warmer, is also cleverer in a way, for he plays on Leo's feelings for Marian. Mrs Maudsley wilfully exposes him – with dire results to herself and Leo. The film shows her shielding him by drawing his head on to her breast away from the sight of the lovers while Marian protectively shields Ted in the same way. The novel conveys briefly the full impact. Even Trimingham innocently contributes to the corruption of innocence, his smoking-room conversation and the 'lady-killer' suggestion worrying the boy who has come into a man's world without understanding it. If the grown-ups, through selfishness and insensitivity, contribute to Leo's loss of innocence, Marcus too has a hand in it. His 'awe-mongers' pun, his leading on of Leo to reveal where Marian is, his teasing of Leo over the meaning of the word 'green', his concern for correct behaviour but his delight in gossip, all these are corrupting influences on his friend.

Central to this is Leo's corruption of himself, the fact that he goes on doing what he senses he should not be doing, that he tells lies and, above all, that having practised his spells with luck he puts faith in them as a positive means of doing good. I have referred elsewhere to his battle with the deadly nightshade, and early in the novel we are told that every part of it is poisonous. Leo, in effect, through plant and superstition, is contaminated within his mind. Leo cannot escape from the spell of Marian, of Ted, of Trimingham's rank and Mrs Maudsley's physical grasp. Nor can he escape from the spell of his imagination, his superstition, his fantasy. When he holds the stump of the plant he holds reality, but reality in life is too much for him.

Society and Class

In giving *The Go-Between* a local and period setting, Hartley is examining and exposing the class prejudices and class attitudes of the time. Some of these are unchanging too, and in country areas of England today there are obvious divisions between the rich and the labourers, the leisured and aristocratic and their servants. In the gathering at the village hall for the concert there is a mingling of classes for this one occasion of the year. But the social differences are more than registered in the audience, those from the hall being treated with deference, while the rest are on their own level of give and take – where Ted, for example, not behaving in his usual manner, can be the object of sarcasm and comment from his fellows.

At the very top of the social scale is Trimingham. The ninth viscount is looked up to by everybody, is spoken of as 'his lordship' by Ted, exercises his patronage in a kindly and gentle way, and is almost certainly hard up. Next come the Maudsleys, Mr Maudsley being a successful city businessman who has made a lot of money. Yet we should notice the differences between the Maudsleys and Trimingham. They are intent on demonstrating that they are socially acceptable by the amount of entertaining that they do, yet their sense of difference is seen in Mrs Maudsley's constantly deferring to Trimingham. They are tenants not owners, and the description of Brandham Hall copied by Leo (pp. 32–3) is an important indication of their position. If Marian marries Trimingham then the Maudsleys are by this connection that much higher up the social scale. That they are uncertain, and that they need the support of Trimingham, is evident except in the case of Mr Maudsley. Marian's pique or Marian being gracious show the two sides of her awareness that she is her family's commercial asset.

But it is on Denys and Marcus that the striking influence of Trimingham's class makes its greatest impact. Denys talks always of Trimingham's taste, for example in ties, while his mention of Goodwood, where, he says, Trimingham would surely be going rather than coming to Brandham, shows his wish to be identified with the habits of this eminently acceptable lord. Marcus's snobbery is also built on insecurity. He knows exactly what should be worn on a given occasion and how to treat servants, while his research into social customs and practice includes the ridiculous assertion that porridge should be eaten by the men while standing up. That Marcus's snobbery derives from his mother there is little doubt, for Mrs Maudsley, while not referring to the smell of the villagers at the concert, obviously disapproves of this mixing. She and Marcus know the servants' secrets. She has a part to play, that of society hostess; her husband too has a part to play, that of local squire making the witty speech before the concert begins.

Into this family comes a boy from a middle-class background. Leo's father, although cultured and having a book collection which later proves to be worth enough for Leo to go on through boarding school, and have a small income throughout life, was content to be a bank manager in Salisbury. His mother had enjoyed such social occasions as visits to that town. Leo at boarding school is at first unhappy and bullied until the spells prove effective. At Brandham he becomes a greater snob. Though Leo is aware that his mother has limited means, he knows that it is desirable to have money. We see this when he tells Marian that he hasn't any money to buy clothes in Norwich. Whereas for Leo money is scarce, at Brandham Hall money is spent on every possible occasion, including Leo's birthday. Faced with this and with meeting a lord, and soon being on familiar terms with that lord, Leo is overcome by social awareness and, since he is accepted, by new social status. Leo's new suit is Leo's new status; he is the messenger of the gods who inhabit Brandham Hall. Trimingham is the aristocratic god who has to marry money; the Maudsleys are the commercial gods and goddesses who, through Mrs Maudsley, are going to ensure that he does so. Leo the outsider tries to absorb the social conventions of the hall.

The striking link between the three classes here is that each is flawed in some way. Trimingham's scars, admittedly acquired in the war, make him less than a complete man, for his family is scarred, it has come down in the world, and it is scarred again when Marian gives birth to a son which is certainly not his. Mrs Maudsley is scarred by her interference in order to preserve what she has set her heart on, a marriage of status for her daughter; she is permanently scarred by mental illness. Leo is scarred by what he suffers and what he sees throughout his life.

Ted Burgess is the social outsider of the novel. A tenant farmer, a 'bit of a lad', a bachelor living alone apart from the woman who comes in to clean for him, Ted represents hard work, a reasonable standard of living, an acceptance of those who are socially above him. He may also represent the coming man of the new century who will breach the class barrier, but in the novel he fails. Marian says that he is weak, and if suicide is weakness then Ted is weak. But the cricket match and the concert show him at his best, apart from those moments with Leo when his kindness to the boy transcends his own needs. His swimming in the bathing place can be seen as an encroachment upon those with privileges. His innings can be seen as a challenge to the hall and aristocratic society. His singing represents his coming together with Marian in full public view. But his time – the period which Leo thinks of as the Golden Age – has not yet come. If Ted and Marian are rebelling against established society, they fail but, significantly, it is Ted's grandson who survives as the eleventh viscount.

The grandson can be seen as helping to bring about 'a healthy merger of the classes', but we should remember – unless Marian is lying – that he wants to marry a Winlove, 'a distant cousin, but still a Winlove' (p. 278). (Winlove is Trimingham's family name.) This is Hartley's final ironic twist, for the Winloves have had Brandham Hall in the family for centuries, and this marriage would ensure an inheritance which constitutes privilege if not power. The old Marian lives for her status as Lady Trimingham, deluding herself that all is well and that she is much visited. The commercial Maudsleys have died off or have been killed in the war, and middle-class Leo has lived on in his bleak life.

Marian is rootedly where her mother wanted her to be, but instead of ascending society she has descended because of her past affair with Ted. Leo has turned to the facts he understands in the context he understands. Both have failed to change in a century of change (we must not forget that the date of the Prologue and Epilogue is 1952). If

Hartley has presented class and society as it was in 1900, he has also given us a studied consideration of what remains of it in 1952.

Other Themes

There are other themes in *The Go-Between*. Eric Brown has argued that Leo is searching for a father figure, and that Trimingham and Ted represent different aspects of this search. Certainly Leo admires and respects Hugh, despite the fact that his own father was a pacifist who had no sympathy for the British cause in the Boer War. Ted too is unlike Leo's dead father, who collected books and led a withdrawn life. Trimingham is kind, but it is from good breeding rather than actual warmth; Ted is kind, concerned that this boy who is ignorant of the facts of life should not learn about them in a way that will harm him. When he learns that Leo's father is dead, Ted is not equal to the demands of explanation. He nerves himself to tell Leo later. Leo responds to Ted and to Trimingham because they represent the zodiacal figures of the Water-Carrier and the Archer, and he doesn't know which he wants to be. He *is* moved by Ted, but he seeks to protect Trimingham.

Society at the turn of the century in *The Go-Between* is leisured and good-living. Hartley shows the comings and goings of the guests, the rituals of family prayers and church-going which have little of practical Christianity about them, and the meals, where so much is not eaten. There is a ritual about almost everything that is done, from the trooping off to the bathing place, or the rather regimented walk down to the cricket field, and what Eric Brown has rightly called the 'pseudo-democracy represented by the Hall cricket-team'. If breakfast is the daily planning ritual, then the birthday tea is the honour-the-guest ritual. Even the concert, unplanned though it seems initially, is a ritual, the various stages of the performance punctuated by comments and movements; the boyish games played by Marcus and Leo are a mockery of a ritual, with the regular pushing and barging and the particular rules of speaking only in French. Leo's spells are, of course, his private ritual. Hartley does not comment on these ritualized lives, for the presentation of them carries its own suggestions of limitation. They are the facts of this dated society life.

SETTING AND PERIOD

The main setting, and the focus of action, is Brandham Hall – its
outhouses, the village cricket ground, the concert hall, and the nearby
Black Farm where Ted lives. There are also the bathing place, a site
for a picnic, the sluice which Leo describes, and a scene of particular
intensity in the gardens of Brandham Hall. There is the trip to Norwich,
with some focus on the cathedral, a mention of particular shops, the
market-place; and there is the older Leo describing his childhood
before boarding school near Salisbury. Interiors are vividly described
throughout, whether in Brandham Hall – consider the main dining-
hall, the staircase, the smoking-room, the bedroom that Marcus and
Leo share and the smaller bedroom to which Leo is transferred when
Marcus is suspected of having the measles. Ted's kitchen is described
to emphasize the contrast between hall and farm in terms of social
foreground and living conditions.

Brandham Hall is in Norfolk about fourteen miles from Norwich
(thirteen and three quarter miles according to Leo) and there is Leo's
transcription from a Norfolk directory (pp. 32–3) as a guide for readers.
Words like 'imposing' (p. 32), 'impressive' (p. 33), plus the description
of the art treasures, and the double staircase, as well as the exterior park
and 'pleasure grounds', all combine to make the main setting the
foreground for the main action of the novel. Leo shows how impressed
he is at the thought of staying in a Georgian mansion, and although he
does indulge in boyish knock-about with Marcus, the fact is that we
get a tremendous sense of *space* both in rooms and grounds. Leo's
imagination is always active. He compares the staircase to 'a tilted
horseshoe, a magnet, a cataract' (p. 33) and is superstitious about it.
The man Leo has forgotten the south-west prospect, but on his return
to Brandham fifty-two years after the childhood events, as he enters the
lodge gates to deliver his final message, the south-west prospect comes
into view. The interior has largely remained in Leo's mind though, and
he recalls 'passages with sudden bends and confusing identical doors'
(p. 33). The sense of place, and the actions associated with that place,
are central to Hartley's conception. The family and their guests are
always on view, and Hartley obviously researched the location and the
period very carefully. The advantages of one major focus are great –
the guests coming and going form a background for the main

drama which is occurring beneath their very eyes, if they did but know it.

The hall represents the self-contained and socially superior set, and Ted Burgess is divided from them by virtue of the fact that he works, is a tenant, and has little education. A river divides his tenanted land from Trimingham's other tenants, the Maudsleys. Ted's security of tenure presumably depends on his landlord's good will, while the tenancy of the Maudsleys will be made more secure if Trimingham marries Marian. He does, and though he is established aristocracy, he is dependent on these tenants, and has responsibilities to them. Hartley is indicating that his settings, like his characters, are connected commercially and economically as well as socially and morally. The setting links the various parts of the novel. When the older Leo returns he goes to the church to inspect the tablets, just as he had done when he was a boy. He is able to deduce what has happened before he meets Marian. But there is change too. Although the settings remain, we note that part of Brandham Hall is now let to a girl's school. The aristocracy and the families raised by their financial status are subject to economic pressures.

The period is firmly 1900, the beginning of the Golden Age envisaged by Leo, the first age of the new world. Hartley's attention to authentic detail runs throughout. There is reference to Eton collars, part of the required dress of public-school boys at this time, and to the landau, the horse-drawn carriage often hired. Boer War (1899–1902) references are thick and fast, with mention of the popular patriotic songs of the time like 'The Soldiers of the Queen' and 'Goodbye Dolly I Must Leave You'. The major event is the capture of Ladysmith, which had been besieged by the Boers for nearly four months before it was relieved by Sir Redvers Buller at the end of February 1900. This was the signal for an outbreak of national rejoicing and expressions of patriotism some five months before the holiday at Brandham Hall. It is topical, precedes Trimingham's meeting with Leo, and shows the contrast between the atmosphere of jingoism (which Leo supported over Ladysmith) and that of pacifism (Leo's father had been pro-Boer).

Other period references are to the use of the bathing machine when the party go for a swim (this could be pushed into the water, a kind of mobile changing hut for the ladies), and to the dress worn by those ladies, not only when they are swimming, but when they are going to play croquet: 'in white, with hourglass figures and hats like windmills'

(p. 35). The men have 'white flannels, white boots ... and straw boaters' (p. 35). If the wider national references embrace the British Commander-in-Chief Lord Roberts and his successor Lord Kitchener in South Africa, as well as mentioning Kruger and de Wet, President of the Transvaal and a Boer general respectively, the local sporting hero of the hour would perhaps be R. E. Foster, the cricketer whose exploits in this particular season included a century in each innings for the Gentlemen against the Players. This was an annual fixture in which the amateurs (gentlemen) played the players (professionals), and in a curiously appropriate sense the hall versus the villagers approximates to this, with Trimingham as the elegant amateur and Ted as the professional hitter. Once again we are conscious of the depth at which L. P. Hartley is working in the interests of genuine period atmosphere.

Leo's return to Brandham Hall means that Hartley has to mention other periods than the chosen one of 1900. The heat of that time (and it was in fact a very hot summer) has been relived through memory. The Leo who sets out in 1952 is now over half way through the century he envisaged as the Golden Age, though for him it has turned out to be the reverse. Hartley conveys the terrible loss of life in the First World War (1914–18), telling us of the death in it of two members of the same family, Marcus and Denys. The 'Golden Age' had an equally terrible Second War (1939–45), and again two members of the family are killed – Ted's son (born seven months after Marian's marriage to Hugh) and his wife, killed in 1941 in an air raid. The century so far has seen much wider tragedies than those with which the narrative has been concerned. Marian, although clinging to the status of the past, has come down in the world. She is living in Nannie Robson's cottage, though for a time she had lived in the Dower House. Hartley's presentation of a distant and fixed period in time is realistic. It doesn't matter whether the reference is to the bicycle, to tights (or bloomers), to the cricketer Gilbert Jessop, to Lord Methuen, to the jokes in *Punch* at the time of the Boer War, to Marian's mention of Liverpool Street: all convey the authentic tone of the period, with the facts of the time that Leo so cherished. It is perhaps the greatest tribute one can pay to Hartley to say that characters, settings and period combine to produce a satisfying and consistent novel.

STRUCTURE

The structure of *The Go-Between* is straightforward. The Prologue and the Epilogue are set in 1952, the main narrative in which a sixty-five-year-old man looks back to an eventful eighteen days in July 1900 comprising twenty-three chapters. The whole novel is told in the first person, the technique employed being that of the supposedly autobiographical narrator. Throughout, the narrator has the advantage of hindsight except in the Epilogue, which is told through flashback to the events immediately after the catastrophe (Leo's breakdown, his return to school, etc.). It is brought up to date in direct narrative with Leo's return to Brandham Hall. The emphasis in the main narrative flashback, that is, the story of Leo's stay at Brandham Hall, is on Leo seen as the events happen to him. The dialogue, for instance, is given with all the immediacy of words spoken now, in the present. Hartley is being very subtle here, and the narrative method is carefully structured so that he can (a) present things as if they were actually happening by entering the consciousness of the boy as he experienced them; and (b) indicating the advantages of the narrator's hindsight fifty-two years on to comment on the nature of the experiences, whether they are Leo's reactions to seeing Ted's body or the emotions he felt/feels in the struggle with the deadly nightshade. The blend of boy and adult reactions is entirely successful, mainly because of the psychological consistency with which Leo is presented.

The structure of the novel is dependent on a strict chronological sequence, and here, as elsewhere, Hartley is accurate and detailed. The diary provides the frame in the same way as Prologue and Epilogue do. On Friday 15 June Leo goes home from school, which has finished early because of the measles outbreak. He notes that Mrs Maudsley's letter arrives on 1 July, 'for in those days we still had a post on Sundays' (p. 29). This is right, since 15 June had been a Friday. She originally suggests 10 July as the date when Leo can go to Brandham Hall, the invitation embracing 'the rest of the month' (p. 29). But Leo arrives on the 9th (a Monday) and presumably breaks down immediately after the outhouse scene (Friday 27 July, his birthday). We learn from the Epilogue that Mrs Colston comes down on the Saturday and has to be put up at the inn. On Sunday (29th) Mr Maudsley assumes charge. Leo stays until the Monday (30 July, p. 276). The experiences which shape a lifetime have taken three weeks to the very day.

Within that chronological structure there are interesting emphases. For example, the Monday (9th) was 'a cool temperate day' (p. 39), the weather in which Leo is at his best before the Brandham experiences. The next day (Tuesday 10th) the thermometer stands at eighty-three (p. 39). Leo begins to feel uncomfortable, his clothes are unsuitable, and he hasn't yet adjusted to his changed circumstances. The comments on his clothes, though kindly meant, upset Leo, and that night he works out a spell to lower the temperature. There is a partial success, but on Thursday (12 July) Marian comes to the rescue, and takes Leo to Norwich the next day (Friday 13th). Trimingham arrives late on Saturday (14th) and Leo sees him at church the next day (Sunday 15th). Leo notes in his diary that the bathing party is on Saturday 14th, which is not a very hot day. Marcus is confined to his room on Sunday (15th) and reveals that the ball for Marian and Trimingham will be held on Saturday (28th).

For almost the first week of his stay, then, Leo is still free, but in talking to Trimingham on that first occasion on the Sunday he volunteers to 'take messages' (p. 72) as a means of showing his devotion to Marian. That same afternoon he slides down Ted's straw-stack and then takes his message. The Monday (16th) is the picnic, while Leo reveals that between Tuesday (17th) and Saturday (21st) 'I three times carried messages between Marian and Ted Burgess: three notes from her, one note and two verbal messages from him' (p. 101). Marcus gets up and cramps Leo's style on Friday 20th. On that day Leo reads Marian's words to Ted. Leo recovers, and excels, on the next day, at the cricket match and the concert. On Sunday 22nd Leo is happy at first, but made very unhappy by Marian's anger at his refusal to take the message later. Ted is exasperated by his insistence on knowing about spooning, Leo writes the second letter of the day to his mother (asking in this one to be recalled home), and afterwards he and Marcus hear the couple spooning. Leo leaves his letter in the box. Marian goes to London on the Monday (23rd). On Tuesday (24th) Leo receives Ted's letter (written on Sunday), and on Wednesday morning (25th) he reads *Punch*. He goes to say goodbye to Ted, believing that this will be his last day. When he returns for tea he finds that his mother has written, but that she will not let him come home. On Thursday morning Mrs Maudsley, who has been ill, appears at breakfast. Leo tells Marian later that Ted may be going to the war. He falsifies the time of Ted's final meeting with Marian, casts his spell, and destroys the belladonna (this probably carries over after midnight on the 26th to the early hours of Leo's birthday, the 27th). On the 27th Leo receives the ties, changes before luncheon (the weather has broken), is afterwards caught in possession of the letter by Mrs Maudsley, attends his birthday tea, is dragged out to search for Marian, and sees her in the outhouse with Ted.

This time sequence gives the action a convincing particularity. The diary records the days, the boy records the experiences, each serving the other. While it reflects the novelist's artistic sense, it also – and this is another level for reader appreciation – reflects the narrator's concern for facts, for accuracy and truthfulness of statement. Throughout the thermometer rises and falls with the temperature of the fictional action. Unlike people, it cannot lie.

NARRATIVE ART

Hartley's narrative art ranges from dialogue to the use of symbols, from natural description to particular images, from explorations of Leo's consciousness to the carrying of messages, from irony to straight statement. There are other aspects of style too, like the use of repetition and schoolboy language, slang, current colloquialisms and, from time to time, the contemporary or learned reference that adds something more to our appreciation of the text.

Dialogue

The Go-Between is rich in dialogue. Some of it is natural and unforced, as between Trimingham and Leo, and between Ted and Leo in a different social context but with sympathetic contact. Sometimes the dialogue is deliberately ironic. By ironic I mean here the difference between how *characters* see a situation and the *reality* of the situation. This kind of irony is present in Leo's sexual ignorance throughout his stay at Brandham Hall. The dialogue between Ted and Leo about spooning is ironic; the dialogue between Marian and Leo when she calls him a 'little Shylock' is ironic, with its cruel effects on Leo. One could go on, because the novel is full of irony throughout. There is also irony in the situations where the reader knows what the character or characters in a novel do not know. We as readers of *The Go-Between* know the facts of life and the meaning of the colloquial terms with which the dialogue is often sprinkled; Leo knows neither.

Hartley is the master of various styles of dialogue. When Trimingham talks with Leo about his ancestor who was killed in a duel, we are aware of the boy's earnest questioning and Trimingham's well-bred, almost clipped delivery which takes all emotion from the situation. Phrases like 'Nothing is ever a lady's fault; you'll learn that', and 'He was a good-looking blackguard, I believe' (p. 161) are at one level the simple dialogue between man and boy. At another level they are ironic when thought of in the context of the future lives of the man and boy, for if 'nothing' is Marian's fault, they must suffer in their separate ways. Always we are impressed by the *range* of the dialogue, and particularly impressive here are the exchanges between Marcus and Leo on a give-and-take schoolboy level. The rules are imposed by Marcus when they speak in French and have made-up and tack-on words or phrases in order not to lose face. Colloquialisms and slang are twin keys to the ironic use of dialogue. Leo does not understand 'lady-killer', 'a bit of a lad', or Marcus's inspired pun 'awe-mongers'. Yet Leo tends to live by words alone (consider the words of the spells in monologue) and is quite a witty boy in his own way.

Letters

If the spoken word is very important in *The Go-Between*, then the written word is certainly as important, and it is often employed with similar ironic effects. There are messages, which form part of the dialogue of the novel. The message can be altered (remember Leo's changing of the time in Ted's final one) or merely repeated, as when Ted says to Leo 'Tell her it's no go' (p. 101). Trimingham's messages are open and simple; Ted's and Marian's are a continuing deception (until he finds out) of Leo and, of course, of Trimingham and Mrs Maudsley. Both Marian and Ted refer to the fact there is 'business' between them, a simple cover-up of their sexual passion, particularly for an innocent boy. But letters are important throughout the novel, and have a varying impact. The first letter from Mrs Maudsley (1 July) with its invitation to Leo to spend the rest of the month at Brandham Hall (after the 10th) sets the whole action in motion and gives some foretaste of the Maudsleys' social status by which Leo is so impressed. We are merely given quotations from this. Other letters form a kind of running commentary on the main action. Marian's unsealed letter is crucial. Leo has only to read what is not hidden – 'Darling, darling, darling, Same place, same time, this evening' (p. 110) – for his emotional life to be shattered.

The dramatic sense of change, Leo's inward turmoil, is nowhere better shown than in the two letters that he writes to his mother on Sunday 22 July, the day after the cricket match and concert triumph. The first is written between breakfast and church and tells of his success and happiness. It is not quoted but merely reported. The second is written (a) after Trimingham's account of his ancestor's death in a duel, (b) after Marian has raged at Leo and accused him of being mercenary, and (c) after Ted has failed to tell Leo exactly what spooning is. That second letter shows Leo driven to near breakdown – and it therefore anticipates his later breakdown after his terrible exposure by Mrs Maudsley. While Marian is absent, Leo lives for his mother's telegram which will summon him home before his birthday. Instead he receives a letter which is remarkable for its lack of understanding, for its complacency, and for its adult incomprehension of a child's suffering.

On the day that Leo writes to his mother, Ted writes to him, though he doesn't receive it until the Tuesday. It is a letter full of remorse. Ted writes, 'I will try and tell you what you asked' (p. 202), but Leo is suspicious. Its timing is important, since Leo fully expects to be away from Brandham before the Sunday on which Ted has invited him to tea. But the last letter is the one which deserves pride of place. Leo does not read it until fifty-two years after his experiences at Brandham, but he is moved to tears when he does. He learns that the bicycle would have made it easier for him to deliver the messages, and that Marian changed the time back to Ted's original suggestion. There is some affection for him in the letter, but there is deep, deep hurt.

The diary is, to a degree, Leo's continuing letter to himself. The bare outlines of print convey the atmospheres and experiences of that magic and disenchanted past. It is the boy's letter which the adult reads. It is the letter which runs the whole length of the novel, and we have the feeling when we finish reading it that no answer is possible, for there is not enough life left in Leo for him to begin one.

SYMBOLS

One of the essential ingredients of *The Go-Between* is the author's use of symbolism in a richly suggestive way. A symbol is quite simply an object which stands for or represents something else, an obvious example in the popular consciousness being the idea that the dove is the symbol of peace. The diary's date symbolizes the Golden Age which Leo sees in the new century. The date itself is surrounded by the signs of the zodiac which, to the young Leo, symbolized the one certain power he had, a power of combatting life when it got out of hand. This had proved effective through his spells in the past, but when Leo arrives at Brandham Hall and meets Marian (the Virgin), Trimingham (the Archer) and Ted (the Water-Carrier), symbol and reality come together in his mind. This is ironic, but it is significant that the zodiacal currents run through Leo's consciousness during the stay, so that the final experience is seen by him and expressed in his own way. Ted and Marian are 'together on the ground, the Virgin and the Water-Carrier, two bodies moving like one' (p. 262).

The main symbol of the novel is the deadly nightshade. It is linked to Marian, who is beautiful but, seen in terms of Leo's immediate and later life, evil. It is linked to Mrs Maudsley for the same reasons. Leo fears for it, feeling that because it is poisonous all over he must not tell Mrs Maudsley about it, since it might then be destroyed, 'its lusty limbs withering on a rubbish-heap' (p. 38). This sexuality in description is matched later by the idea of the *Atropa belladonna* seeming to reach out from the outhouse and beckoning Leo into its embrace. The actual scene in which Leo destroys it has sexual suggestions. But the boy is still innocent and still practises his spell in order to eliminate Ted from the situation. In killing the nightshade Leo helps to bring about his own death of the spirit, the death of Marian's and Ted's love, Ted's physical death as the result of discovery, and the death of Mrs Maudsley's sanity. The plant symbolizes beauty, evil and power.

But if the plant is the natural symbol of what is corrupt and destructive, then the associations of green with Leo symbolize his innocence, his fantasy, his capacity to divide the precious present of his life at Brandham from his limited past. Marian's present makes her Maid Marian and Leo becomes Robin Hood; the bicycle which Leo never rides is also green, and would have helped him to continue as deceived go-between. The green suit gives Leo the freedom he wants, but again we are aware of the irony which marks his every action and reaction. To put it simply, wearing green means that Leo is free to be green. Marcus's malice here hurts Leo with its suggestion that Marian deliberately chose the colour because of Leo's simplicity and ignorance.

The heat has a strongly symbolic effect. Leo fears it and wishes to eliminate it by spells – he has suffered from it before and in his Norfolk suit it seems as if he will suffer again. But Marian's gift makes the heat his friend, and on one occasion he thinks perhaps the heat is Marian. This is very important, for in the sexual sense heat stimulates passion, love-making, with the sun as the great giver of life and vitality. Yet even here the symbol is used ironically. It makes Leo a 'new' person, and he has triumphs during its rule (like the cricket match). It gives him awareness but not knowledge. It rouses interest but it also wounds. At moments of Leo's experience it is always in evidence, as when he is moved by seeing Ted's body at the bathing place. The Leo of the future who will give his life to facts is seen already in the Leo who goes to the game-larder to regularly check the thermometer. That fact registers daily, just as the messages and the experiences register in Leo's consciousness.

Signals of a change in the weather appear as early as the cricket match, when Leo's attention is caught by a particular cloud: 'Was there a menace in this purple tract, a hint of thunder? I did not think so' (p. 134). As so often, Leo is wrong, but it is not until his birthday that the full force of the menace is unleashed. The projected visit to Beeston Castle has to be abandoned, and as Mrs Maudsley cross-questions Leo the rumbling of the thunder brings an end to his immediate suffering. But the storm is gathering, the darkness is such that the lights are lit for the birthday tea, and Leo is swept out into the downpour by Mrs

Maudsley. They reach the outhouses sodden, and Leo records his awareness of 'the indescribable smell of rain filling the air' (p. 261). The weather has broken, and breakdown follows.

There is another kind of symbolic rumbling which registers directly in the novel. Throughout the text there are scattered references to the Boer War in South Africa. There Trimingham is wounded, there Ted might have been persuaded to go; Leo, in an intelligent comparison, sees the villagers as the Boers and the hall as the English fighting them The hall just triumphs, but only just, and perhaps the suggestion is that the battle between the classes, seen in miniature in this cricket match, is to be fully joined, just as the battle to hold the Empire will be joined in the coming century. Military imagery is used in this chapter, imagery which would be current in time of war (which this was), but it is not just the imagery of a patriotic boy. For Leo, whose father was a pacifist and a pro-Boer, is divided in his loyalties between Trimingham and Ted. The latter wins in terms of scoring 50 and in having Marian's love (and, I suppose, in siring the son whose son in turn causes Marian so much heartbreak), but Trimingham survives to marry Marian, his title and line continued through Ted.

Another interesting symbolic usage is that of song. Like the letters, the text is sprinkled with songs which set up associations. 'Take a Pair of Sparkling Eyes' obviously expresses the attraction of Marian for Ted and Trimingham, while the song by Balfe with its 'infidelities to come' (p. 144) is a comment on the affair between Ted and Marian which, unlike their singing together, is not out in the open. Leo's sacred song is just as suggestive, for though Marian does not suffer a fate worse than death, in a sense Leo later does, while the refrain 'Clad in robes of virgin white' reflects Leo's innocent view of Marian. Marian singing 'Home, Sweet Home' is a signal that she accepts her marriage, though it is somewhat ironic that she, who does not really value her home and her comforts as much as her love for Ted, should sing it. There are other songs which echo symbolically in *The Go-Between*, such current patriotic songs as 'Goodbye, Dolly Gray', and 'Soldiers of the Queen'. The first has the poignant anticipation of what doesn't happen – Ted going to war – and the second has what did happen to one of the soldiers of the Queen – the scarred Trimingham.

GENERAL

The variety of the language, from Trimingham's well-bred usage to Marcus's French and pseudo-French, has been noted. We should also note (a) the fine description, whether it be of the house, its interiors, the church interior, or some exteriors which make a particular impression on Leo, like the pool which 'had been untidy, now it was a scene of mad disorder: a tangled mass of water-weeds, all high and dry, and, sticking out from them, mounds of yellow gravel, like bald patches on a head' (p. 168). There is a certain prophetic note about the 'scene of mad disorder' to come, but note the imaginative 'like bald patches on a head'. (b) Note too the suddenly arresting and appropriate imagery – Hartley is the master of the economic simile or metaphor, as in Marian being 'like an enchantress' (p. 168) or of Leo himself being 'caught like a moth in the beam from her eye, that black searchlight' (p. 49). (c) There is a marked prophetic element in *The Go-Between*, done in a casual way. Perhaps the best example is when Leo comes upon Ted holding the gun in his kitchen: 'The muzzle was just below his mouth, the barrel was pressed against his naked chest ...' (p. 170). This is a clever anticipation of Ted's forthcoming suicide. (d) Leo always has a methodical mind, and is particularly careful about organizing his spells. Factual language to indicate the exactness of the experiment is used, even to the listing of the utensils which 'must be held in readiness' (p. 238). (e) Contrasting with this there is the fevered language of Leo's consciousness. There is his terror when he begins to tear the deadly nightshade, the curious sensation of seeing himself as another figure when he leaves Marian on his way to the farm after she has denounced him, or the spiritual excitement he feels when he is singing accompanied by Marian. (f) Finally there is the range of reference which runs throughout the novel. It is a language of wide culture – though he had denied himself sexual life, the man Leo has not denied himself other kinds of knowledge. Leo the boy has the interests of Leo the man, and these interests reflect a person of culture. For example, there is the association of Mrs Maudsley with a portrait by Ingres or Goya, there are both biblical and Shakespearean references (apart from the obvious one to Shylock), and there are Leo's personal associations with Icarus. Hartley's style has the measure, balance and interests of the cultivated individual. This is not to identify Leo with his creator, but merely to suggest that Leo's own culture mirrors that of his creator.

The Film of The Go-Between

The film version of *The Go-Between* (1971) was directed by Joseph
Losey, with the screenplay by Harold Pinter. It is available on video,
and well worth seeing. It is beautifully photographed (primarily at
Melton Hall in Norfolk), the heat conveyed by, among other things,
the buzzing of insects. Outdoor shots vie with the interior of Brandham
Hall for pride of place. Ted's farm is visually right, while the cricket
match and the concert convey the falsely-democratic atmosphere which
characterizes the novel on these occasions. The interaction of past
and present is genuinely conveyed by shots from the present being
sandwiched between those of the past, the rain of the present contrasting
symbolically with the almost unbearable heat of the past. The direction
and the script, like the acting, are distinguished, and the film is true to
the spirit of the book. Harold Pinter has an exquisite feeling for words
and, although he retains much of Hartley's dialogue intact, he makes
some interesting alterations which the alert student will notice. The
outhouse scene at the end of the narrative proper also contains a
brilliantly visual shot of Mrs Maudsley and Marian finely aware of each
other at the moment of discovery. The period flavour is sensitively
conveyed, down to such detail as Leo's suit, the boys' accents and slang,
and the swimming party. Do not try to make the film a substitute for
the book, but see it if you can as a genuinely imaginative creation arising
from the novel itself.

Glossary

PERIOD, COLLOQUIAL, LITERARY, CULTURAL REFERENCES

A.1.: First-rate (slang).

Altitude: Height, sublime (feeling).

Ancient Mariner: *The Rime of the Ancient Mariner*, by S. T. Coleridge, where the Mariner tells the story of his trials and tribulations after killing the albatross.

Angels Ever Bright and Fair: From an oratorio by Handel (1750).

Aquarius: The Water-Carrier (Latin).

Atropa Belladonna: The Latin name for the deadly nightshade, meaning beautiful lady, atropa being derived from one of the Greek Fates.

Bags: Claim (slang).

Bags: Trousers (slang)

Balfe: M. W. Balfe, the composer of operas, most famous of which was *The Bohemian Girl* (1843).

Bally: Bloody (slang).

Bathing Machine: Hut for changing in which could be pushed into the water.

Bit of a lad: Always likes being in the company of women (slang).

Black Arts: Magic.

Bloomer: Mistake.

Bloomers: Women's loose baggy knickers, usually gathered in above the knee.

Blub: Cry (slang).

Bluebeard: The villain of a story which was published at the end of the 17th century. He killed his six wives.

Boer(s): South African farming communities who came originally from Holland and who were trying to achieve self-government, hence their fight against the British.

Bosshots: Failures.

Bowdlerize: To eliminate sexual or unfitting references. Derived from Dr Thomas Bowdler, who in 1818 produced a heavily cut version of Shakespeare.

Breaks: Brakes (horse-drawn carriages). Leo's misspelling.

Brougham: Closed horse-drawn carriage.

Browne: Sir Thomas Browne (1605–82), the doctor who lived in Norwich and wrote *Religio Medici* (1643), *A Doctor's Faith*.

Cads: People who don't behave as gentlemen should.

Call out: Challenge (to a duel).

Cat: Be sick (slang).

Chap-fallen: Down in the mouth, depressed.

Claude: Claude Gelles (1600–1682), French painter.

Cricket: It wasn't cricket, i.e. it wasn't the accepted way to behave.

Cripes: Christ (slang).

Crocodile: The usual way children walked when taken from one place to another – in pairs.

Croquet: A game for two to four players who strike a wooden ball through iron hoops with mallets in order to hit a peg.

Cuyp: Albert Cuyp (1620–91), Dutch painter of landscapes.

Danaan: Greek.

David: The young shepherd boy who kills Goliath (I Samuel 17:19–58).

Dead ground: i.e. hidden from view.

Delenda est Belladonna: The belladonna must be destroyed.

De Wet: Christian Rudloph de Wet, leading Boer general.

Dog-cart: Cart with two wheels and two seats back to back.

Dog Days: July/August, the hottest days of the year.

Dog-eared: Turned down (the corner of the page).

Dorm: Dormitory.

Dr Livingstone: David Livingstone, the medical missionary who discovered the Victoria Falls.

Egg: Person (slang).

Eleventh Commandment: A non-existent commandment which would destroy the effect of the other ten, since it is supposed to mean 'Thou shalt not be found out.'

Eton Collars: Broad white collars stiffened. They were not part of the shirt and were worn by public school boys generally in the period, not just those at Eton.

Fairy Ring: Circles of darker grass, superstitiously thought to be so because fairies have been dancing there.

Familiar: A witch's attendant, servant.

Fast: Of loose morals (sexually).

Foster: R. E. Foster, fine amateur cricketer of the period who played for Oxford University, Worcestershire and England.

Gainsborough: Thomas Gainsborough (1727–88), celebrated portrait painter.

Game-larder: Where game was kept cool until it was ready to eat.

Golden Age: The primary ideal age of the world in Greek and Roman mythology.

Goliath: The champion of the Philistines killed by David. He was a giant.

Goodwood: One of the race meetings which would be attended by high society, held annually in July at Goodwood near Chichester.

Goya: Francisco Jose Goya y Lucientes (1746–1826), Spanish portrait painter.

Haha: A ditch which divides the lawn from the park.

Handel: George Frederick Händel, the great German composer of oratorios. He came to England in 1712, and died in 1759 after a very successful career as composer to the court.

Hard Cheese: Bad luck (slang).

Hercules: The hero of Greek myth who possessed phenomenal strength and was called upon to perform a number of labours.

Hobbema: Meindert Hobbema (1638–1709), Dutch painter.

Hole and Corner: Secret and dishonest.

Holler: Utter a loud cry (slang).

'Home, Sweet Home': The very popular song is from the opera *Clari* (1823) by H. R. Bishop and J. H. Payne.

Hottentot: Native of Southern Africa.

Hush-money: Payment for keeping a secret.

Icarus: The son of Daedalus. The latter made him wings which he used to escape from his prison in Crete. He flew too near the sun, the wings were scorched and the wax holding them in place melted. Icarus fell and was drowned.

Impots: Impositions (slang).

Ingres: Jean Auguste Ingres (1781–1867).

In Your Pocket: Under your control (slang).

Jacob's ladder: The ladder Jacob saw had angels going up and down it (Genesis 28:12).

Janus: God of doors and gates in Roman legend.

Jessop: Gilbert Jessop, famous quick-scoring batsman of the period (like Ted, he was a hitter).

Jingo: Agressive patriot.

Kitchener: Lord Kitchener, British Commander-in-Chief against the Boers 1900–1902.

Knocks One Up: Makes you feel very ill (slang).

Kruger: Paulus Kruger, President of the Transvaal (South Africa) republic 1883 99.

L.R.A.M.: Licentiate of the Royal Academy of Music.

Lacuna: Gap.

Ladysmith: Town in Natal, South Africa, besieged by the Boers and relieved on 28 February 1900.

Landau: Four-wheeled carriage.

Loose Balls: i.e. inaccurate bowling in cricket.

Lor Lumme: Lord love me.

Methuen: Lord Methuen, a commander in the Boer War 1899 1902.

Middle and Leg: The batsman would hold his bat straight so that it was between the middle stump and the stump nearest to him.

Midian: The hosts of Midian, enemies of the Israelites in the Old Testament

Ministering Children: Books of stories embodying strict morality by Maria Charlesworth, published in 1854.

Motley: The dress of the court jester.

N.C.O.: Non-commissioned officer.

Norfolk Jacket: Jacket with pleats in front and back.

Olympian: Superior (like the Greek Gods on Mount Olympus).

On the cards: Likely to occur.

On the Square: Reliable, straight.

Outhouses: Building near to, but separate from, main buildings.

Pascal: Blaise Pascal (1623–62), French philosopher, mathematician and author of the famous *Pensées*.

Pax: Truce (slang).

Peau de Chagrin: Balzac's novel, the English translation being *The Wild Ass's Skin* (1831).

Pepys's: Samuel Pepys (1633–1703), who kept a famous diary from 1660 to 1669.

Pi: Pious (slang).

Plebs: Plebeians, lower classes.

Pot-luck: (accepting) whatever there is.

Pretoria: The Boer capital, captured in June 1900.

Puck: The fairy, full of mischief, who is employed by Oberon, King of the Fairies, in Shakespeare's *A Midsummer Night's Dream*.

Pull it off: i.e. win.

Punch: The illustrated weekly magazine, emphasis on humour, was founded in 1841.

Put-up job: Something fake or false.

Quackery: Fake skill or ability.

Quite-quite: Acceptable.

Rag out: Lost temper.

Requiescat: May he rest (Latin).

Revenant: Someone who has come back from being dead.

Reynolds: Sir Joshua Reynolds (1723–92), celebrated portrait painter.

Roberts: Lord Roberts, British Commander-in-Chief against the Boers in 1899–1900.

Ruddy: Bloody (slang).

Run out: Did not complete (his) ground between the wickets.

Ruysdael: Jacob van Ruysdael (1628?–82), Dutch painter.

Sagittarius: The Archer (Latin).

Salisbury. The county town of Wiltshire.

San: Sanatorium.

Sanskrit: The language in which the Ancient Hindu writings are set down.

Season: Society went to London for some weeks in the summer, this period being called the 'season'.

Seedy: Feeling unwell (slang).

Sell: Terrible disappointment (slang).

Set: Established.

Shibboleths: From Judges 12:5–6. Tests to find out if somebody is in the same class as you are.

Shylock: The Jewish moneylender who tries to get his pound of flesh in Shakespeare's *The Merchant of Venice* but is outwitted by Portia.

Side: Superiority (affected) (slang).

Skivvies: Women servants of the lowest rank.

Spartan: Very brave (derived from the inhabitants of Sparta in ancient Greece noted for their courage).

Spifflicating: Outstanding (slang).

Spooning: Cuddling, kissing, making love.

Sport: Wear (slang).

Stand: Buy (slang).

Stanley: Henry Stanley, explorer, journalist, sent out to search for Livingstone in Africa in 1871 by his paper, the *New York Herald*.

Sub: Substitute.

Temenos: Sacred enclosure (Greek).

Teniers: David Teniers the Younger (1610–90), Flemish artist.

'The Minstrel Boy': A famous song with words by the Irish poet Thomas Moore.

Threadneedle Street: Home of the Bank of England in London.

Tin-pot: Of little value.

Togs: Clothes (slang).

Topping: Outstanding (slang).

Transvaal: South African province.

Twelfth Man: Reserve (in cricket) who can be called upon to field but not bat or bowl.

Ulysses: The King of Ithaca in Greek mythology. Only he had the strength to draw his bow.

Ushers: Assistant teachers.

Wild Oats: the name of a horse, but sowing wild oats means living freely, enjoying yourself (sexually) before getting married.

Zodiac: Astronomers in ancient times divided the area covered by the sun in the course of the year into twelve equal parts. Each had a sign with a particular signifi-

cance. (Leo refers to them.)
Zounds: God's wounds, an oath.

FRENCH WORDS AND PHRASES USED IN *THE GO-BETWEEN*

Amour propre: Pride in oneself, esteem.
Aperitif: Alcohol taken before a meal in order to promote the appetite.
Au fond: Basically.
Bonsoir: Good evening.
Bon! Vous venez sur!: Good. You're improving.
C'est une bicyclette: It's a bicycle.
Ça serait trop ennuyeux. Laissons-les faire: That would be too boring. Let's leave them to get on with it.
Cadeau: Present.
Ce n'est pas seulement ça. C'est Marianne: It's not only that. It's Marian.
Cela dépend: That depends.
Certes, c'est pas la patte d'une dame. Mystère. Que dira Maman? Elle a un peur des voleurs!: Certainly, it's a woman's footprint. Some mystery! What will mother say? She has a great fear of thieves.
Clou: Star turn.
Crétin: Idiot.
Déranger: Disturb.
De rigueur: The right thing to do, required by good manners.
Détente: Relaxation.
Deux mois, trois mois: Two months, three months.
Eh bien, je jamais! Well, I never!
Eh bien, je jamais! C'est un couple: Well, well, I never. It's a couple.
En ce moment elle est au lit avec forte migraine, le résultat de tous ces jours de strain: At this moment she is in bed with severe migraine, the result of all these days of tension.
En part, parce que, comme toute les femmes, elle a besoin des habits neufs pour le bal; mais en grand part, à cause de vous, vous . . .: Partly because, like all women, she needs new clothes for the ball, but mainly because of you, you . . .
Entendez vous, coquin? Comprenez vous, nigaud?: Do you hear, rascal? Do you understand, idiot?
Et quant à vos sales pensées, crapaud, je m'en fiche d'elles, je crache: And as for your filthy thoughts, toad, I don't care about them at all, I spit.
Et savez-vous pourquoi?: And do you know why?
Façon de parler: Manner of speaking.
Folle – fou: Mad – mad.
Force majeure: Strong compulsion.
Il est un pea provincial, vous savez: It's somewhat provincial, you know.
Il s'agît des financailles, vous savez. Ma mère n'est sûre que Marianne . . .: It's about the engagement, you know. My mother isn't sure that Marian . . .
Je dirai à Maman que nous avons vu le spoor de Man Friday: I shall tell mother that we have seen Man Friday's footprints.
Je jure: I swear.
Je le trouve trop ennuyeux: I find it too boring.
Je n'aime pas votre voix: I don't like your voice.
Je ne dis pas ça aux petits garçons: I don't tell little boys that

Je ne l'ai pas vue: I haven't seen it.

Je ne sais pas: I don't know.

Je sais bien: I certainly do know.

Je suggère que nous visitons les outhouses: I suggest that we visit the outhouses.

Je vois l'empreinte d'un pied: I see a footprint.

Jurez, jurez, je vous en prie: Swear, swear that you won't, I beg you.

Les convenances: Conventional practices.

Les petits garçons: Little boys.

Mais les chandelles: But the candles.

Mais non: But no.

Mais non! Elle est trè nerveuse! C'est un type un peu hystérique: But no. She is very neurotic. She is a rather hysterical person.

Mais non! Quand je suis parti, la Marianne n'était pas encore arrivée. Et la pauvre Robson était bien facheuse: No. When I left Marian hadn't turned up yet. And poor Miss Robson was quite worried.

Mais oui! Quelle bonne idée. Ce sont des places delicieuses: But yes! What a good idea. They are delightful places.

Mais pourquoi avez-vous perdu la langue?: But why have you lost your tongue?

Mais oui! Vraiment!: But yes! Truly!

Mais les chandelles: But the candles.

Mon pauvre imbécile: My poor fool.

Ne voudriez-vous pas savoir: Wouldn't you like to know.

Oombaire: Humber.

Ou Mademoiselle Friday: Or Miss Friday's.

Outré: Way out, beyond what is acceptable.

Parce que vous êtes vous-même: Because you are (green) yourself.

Pas cent lieues d'ici: Not a hundred leagues from here.

Pas comme il faut – entièrement défendu: Not the proper thing – absolutely forbidden.

Peau de Chagrin: The Wild Ass's Skin (novel by Balzac, 1799–1850).

Perdu sa mémoire: Lost her memory.

Planté là: Left in the lurch.

Pourquoi?: Why?

Sa mémoire est aussi bonne que la mienne, et cent fois meilleure que la vôtre: Her memory is as good as mine, and a hundred times better than yours.

Saignant: Bloody.

Sales types: Offensive people.

Savez-vous où est Marianne en ce moment-ci?: Do you know where Marian is at this moment?

Savoir-faire: Having the ability to do the right thing (in any situation).

Si vous le pouvez: If you can do so.

Un couple qui fait le cuiller: A couple who are spooning.

Un petit quart d'heure: A few minutes.

Un vert fif: A bright green.

Vis-à-vis: With reference to.

Vous avez vu votre soeur chez Mademoiselle Robson?: Did you see your sister at Nannie Robson's?

Vous êtes très silencieux: You are very quiet.

Vous venez sur!: You are coming on!

Vous voudriez dire la belladonne, n'est pas?: You would like to speak about the deadly nightshade, is that so?

Examination Questions

1. How important is the idea of magic in *The Go-Between*?

2. 'Marian should be regarded with sympathy and compassion'.
Discuss her motives and actions as if you were a friend of hers.

3. Show how, throughout the book, Leo's background is contrasted
with the way of life at Brandham. What effects does this contrast have
on him?

(*Southern Universities Joint Board, 1979*)